HELP GOD TO HELP YOU

WHATEVER YOU DO
DO IT WITH A SMILE

SIRSHREE

Help God to Help You
Whatever you do, do it with a smile

By **Sirshree** Tejparkhi

Copyright © Tejgyan Global Foundation
All Rights Reserved 2021

Tejgyan Global Foundation is a charitable organization
with its headquarters in Pune, India.

ISBN : 978-81-8415-333-0

Published by WOW Publishings Pvt. Ltd., India

First Edition published in Jan 2011

Second Edition published in May 2013

Fifth Reprint published in Mar 2025

Printed and bound by Trinity Academy For Corporate Training Ltd, Pune

Copyright and publishing rights are vested exclusively with WOW Publishings Pvt. Ltd. This book is sold subject to the condition that it shall not by way of trade or otherwise, be lent, resold, hired out, or otherwise circulated without the publisher's prior written consent in any form of binding or cover other than that in which it is published and without a similar condition including this condition being imposed on the subsequent purchaser and without limiting the rights under copyright reserved above, no part of this publication may be reproduced, stored in or introduced into a retrieval system, or transmitted, in any form, or by any means, electronic, mechanical, photocopying, recording or otherwise, without the prior written permission of both the copyright owner and the above-mentioned publisher of this book. Any person who does any unauthorized act in relation to this publication may be liable to criminal prosecution and civil claims for damages.

Although the author and publisher have made every effort to ensure accuracy of content in this book, they hereby disclaim any liability to any party for any loss, damage, or disruption caused by errors or omissions, resulting from negligence, accident, or any other cause. Readers are advised to take full responsibility to exercise discretion in understanding and applying the content of this book.

This book is dedicated to all those comedians,
who face untold sufferings in their personal lives
and yet spread laughter with their antics.

Contents

	Preface	7
1.	The Biggest Helper	15
2.	The Guide: Why Only God?	19
3.	Seven Obstacles In Receiving Divine Guidance	22
4.	Seven Ways to Prepare Ourselves for Receiving Divine Guidance	28
5.	Seven Steps of Guidance First Step: Form a relationship with God	33
6.	Second Step: Whatever You Do, Do It With A Smile	38
7.	Third Step: Unlocking	45
8.	Fourth Step: Become Newton And Learn Something New	50
9.	Fifth Step: Awaken The Wise Inner Voice	56
10.	Sixth Step: Become A Plain Paper	62
11.	Seventh Step: Learn to Wait	68

12. How To Receive Divine Guidance	78
13. Recognize The Sign Language	83
14. When Does God Laugh?	91
15. God Laughs Or Cries: Depending Upon Your Faith In Him	95
16. Man's Inherent Nature: Laughter	98
17. First Laughter: Lip Laughter	102
18. Second Laughter: Head Laughter	105
19. Third Laughter: Heart Laughter	110
20. Laughter Experiment	112
21. Learn To Laugh At Your Fears and Your Anger	114
22. First Laughter And Discipline	117
23. Expression of Laughter	125
24. Laughter And Health	127
Divine Guidance	130
Appendices	133

Preface

Only One Mantra

'*Read jokes with laughter*'—one generally understands this advice, but '*Whatever you do, do it with a smile*' is not something that appeals to everyone's intellect. However, this is the mantra which is the main focus of this book and also it is the mantra for you which can help you lead a happy life.

If you read this book with a happy frame of mind, it will become a gift of wisdom for you. What happens when you give a gift to someone? That someone becomes happy. Then his happiness encourages you to buy more gifts for him in the future. On the other hand, what if that person does not express any happiness and does not give any importance to your gift… instead he keeps it aside with a sour face? Sure enough, you won't feel like giving him any more gifts. This is what happens with spiritual guidance as well. It is a divine gift. It is not one of your possessions, nor is it one of your ideas. It is God's guidance, which you receive through insights and intuitions. You must always be grateful for this gift and you must always convey your gratitude to God for it. Your gratitude will ensure non-stop supply of such guidance in future as well. If you don't feel grateful, you will stop receiving this priceless gift.

God wants everybody on this Earth to live happily. That is why He created this beautiful world. Every father wishes happiness for his children, despite all the problems that they may encounter in their daily lives.

> There was a man who always grumbled about his problems. One day he met a spiritual master and requested, 'Please suggest me a place where there are no problems.' The master replied, 'I know of one such place where hundreds of people stay together but no one has any problems whatsoever.' The man was delighted to hear this. 'I would love to stay there. Please take me there as soon as possible.' The master led him into a large graveyard and said, 'This is the place where there are hundreds of people with no problems at all.'

Problems are an inherent part of life; they will continue as long as we live. Consider them to be lessons, challenges or stepping stones, which are crucial for our overall growth. We should not stop being happy because of our problems and stay in ignorance and suffering.

We usually live our lives in the darkness of ignorance and suffering. When the light of Truth dawns, that's when we awaken from our unconsciousness and ignorance. As we receive guidance from the Source of this light (God/Consciousness), we begin to lead a real and joyful life, while spreading laughter among all. That's when we embody the mantra: *Whatever you do, do it with a smile.*

Let us read an enlightening tale. Once upon a time, hundreds of owls lived in a garden. This garden was in complete shambles. You could see the owls hanging from the branches of the trees with long, gloomy faces. There was not a sign of joy in sight. One evening a swan flew into the garden and started chatting with the owls. One of the owls asked the swan, 'Who are you? How do you look so happy! What makes you happy?'

As soon as the owl asked this question, tears started flowing from the eyes of all the other owls. Their faces were pathetic, as if asking, 'Why is there no joy in our lives? Why are we inundated with sorrow?'

The swan replied, 'When you see the light, you too will become happy, and start smiling and laughing like me.'

The owls were surprised and asked, '*Light!* What is that? What does it look like? We have heard this word for the first time.'

Now it was the swan's turn to be surprised. 'You don't know what is light?! We receive light from the sun.'

The word 'sun' was also new for the owls. They asked, 'What is *sun*?'

The swan was shocked. 'What?! You don't know the sun? When the sun rises, the darkness of night vanishes and the day begins.'

The owls were clueless. 'What is *day*? This word too is foreign to us.'

The swan couldn't believe this. 'You don't even know about the day! The day appears when the sun rises. In a week of a human calendar there is a day called Sunday. Sunday means sun and day. If you bathe in sunlight on a Sunday, you will experience the same joy which I am experiencing. The same laughter, which has brightened my face, will brighten yours too.'

The owls could not understand the swan. So, they told him, 'We shall ask our elders about this. They will tell us the truth.'

The owls then approached their elders and said, 'We've just met a swan who says that all our troubles shall vanish and we will attain unlimited joy if we bathe in the glory of sunlight. What is your opinion on this?' The elders reacted sharply. 'That's nonsense! There is no truth in it. There is no word called *light* in the owl dictionary. There is no such joy in the owls' lives that the swan is talking about. He is absolutely

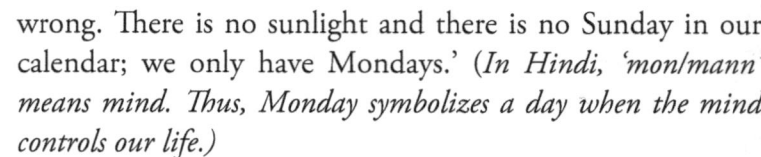

wrong. There is no sunlight and there is no Sunday in our calendar; we only have Mondays.' (*In Hindi, 'mon/mann' means mind. Thus, Monday symbolizes a day when the mind controls our life.*)

After listening to their elders, the owls concluded that indeed there is no such thing as light. They came back and told the swan, 'You lied and tried to fool us. There is no such light anywhere. There is no Sunday and there is no sunlight, which can change an owl into a swan by bathing in it. These are bookish stories, and that too from your books; our holy books do not mention any of this. We are sorry but we don't trust you at all.'

The swan calmly replied, 'If you wish to directly experience the truth, I shall call out to you in the morning and make you experience it. All you have to do is open your eyes on hearing my call. You then won't need to take my word for it. You will see everything on your own and that will put all arguments to rest. You will experience the light and the sun and know what a day is. You will know the truth at the experiential level as soon as the light appears.'

This was highly unusual and completely against the owl tradition. However, some owls got ready to experiment. They agreed to wake up on being called.

At the crack of dawn, the swan called out to those owls. The call woke them up and for the first time they encountered sunlight. They also experienced what is true happiness and real laughter. They understood how to smile. They learnt how to do everything with a smile and become a swan. In fact, for the first time they realized that they were not owls... but were actually swans! They had forgotten their true identity because they had closed their eyes to light.

The same thing happens with us. As soon as we hear something new, we reject it straightaway. This story teaches us that if someone is providing guidance to us based upon personal experience, the least we can do is listen. We should not reject it immediately. We should try to look at it from a new viewpoint. We can understand the swan's perspective only by being a swan. If you are being told that there is a new and beautiful way of leading your life, *listen* to it with an open mind. The light (wisdom), sun and day are all inside you. Don't dismiss this thought right away. Experience it firsthand and learn the mantra of permanent happiness. Nature is always ready to provide you with such guidance.

Man needs guidance at every turn of his life—be it childhood, teenage, adulthood or old age. A child needs his parents' guidance, a student needs his teachers' guidance, a disciple needs his master's guidance and a devotee needs God's guidance. You easily get guidance from parents and teachers, and with its help you can reach a high stature in life. But when you receive divine guidance, that is when miracles start happening in your life and you reach the pinnacle of success.

Let us take another example. A man was to travel by an airplane. He reached the airport and was about to board his flight when he heard a little voice from inside him asking him to get down and not to travel by that plane. It was a soft voice, and it was not supported by any logic. He couldn't understand this. After some deliberation, he decided to heed the voice and got off the plane. After a few hours he came to know that the airplane, which he had almost boarded, had met with a serious accident. Now what was that? That voice was guidance received through intuition from the Self, Consciousness or God within us—whatever you choose to believe. Remember, there was no logic in it; it was just a little inner voice. This inner voice can urge us to undertake or reject a given thing. We all need this guidance. You will receive this guidance from this book. This book is going to guide you to recognize and listen to that inner voice—the guidance from God.

Only happy people can recognize and receive this divine guidance, and thereby only they can spread happiness to others. The unhappy ones keep complaining all their lives and do not even realize what a precious gift they are missing out on. They never come to know that only one mantra could have led the boat of their lives ashore. This mantra was, is and shall remain: *Whatever you do, do it with a smile.*

This mantra will help you receive divine guidance. That will in turn help you to attain joy and learn the art of loving unconditionally. This art will help you become an expert in receiving divine guidance. So, what are you waiting for? Whatever you read, read it with a smile.

Section I

How to Receive Guidance from God

*Just as many a time you wish to be alone
with your own self,
God too wishes to spend some time alone
with you every day.
Therefore, please spend some time daily with God
through prayer and meditation.*

Chapter 1

The Biggest Helper
The Highest Guide

God is constantly guiding us through various channels, but we are unable to understand His signals. As a result we remain devoid of His invaluable guidance and lead a life of suffering.

Have total faith in the fact that God is always with you—during happy times as well as challenging times. His presence is not like that of worldly folks who stick with you during joys but abandon you during sorrows. God is your true companion. The following story illustrates this fact.

> One night a man had a dream. He dreamed he was walking along the beach with the Lord. Across the sky flashed scenes from his life. For each scene he noticed two sets of footprints in the sand: one belonging to him, and the other to the Lord.
>
> When the last scene of his life flashed before him, he looked back at the footprints in the sand. He noticed that many times along the path of his life there was only one set of footprints.
>
> He also noticed that it happened at the very lowest and saddest times in his life. This really bothered him and he questioned the Lord about it: "Lord, you said that once

I decided to follow you, you'd walk with me all the way. But I have noticed that during the most troublesome times in my life, there is only one set of footprints. I don't understand why when I needed you most you would leave me."

The Lord replied: "My son, my precious child, I love you and I would never leave you. During your times of trial and suffering, when you see only one set of footprints, it was then that I carried you."

God is always with us and He lives in every heart. He communicates with us through the small inner voice. But as our mind remains preoccupied with thoughts, we are unable to hear this voice. God has always been trying to guide us but we haven't been able to understand it owing to our ignorance. Let us further understand this through a fable.

Once upon a time, some clouds approached God and said, 'We quench the Earth's thirst during the rainy season by soaking it with water. In the process, we also provide relief to the world from scorching heat. We help give life to everything. But we do this job for just four months in a year. During the remaining months, we roam around idly doing nothing. Please give us an opportunity to be of service to people during this idle period.' God smiled and said, 'Dear Clouds, your idea of service is very noble. From now on, you will become my messengers. Convey my messages to people by forming words in the sky. Give them the message of what they should do in their life and what they should learn from nature. If they wish to know about their future, convey that as well.'

The clouds were ecstatic. They thought, 'This is indeed a noble deed. Now we can alleviate the suffering of all human beings. We will give them suitable and timely messages, so that they will never do anything wrong. And then the Earth will become Heaven.' They began their work with zeal and zest. They saw a man walking down the street. There was a ditch at the turning on the road ahead. The clouds immediately got into action. They scattered themselves and formed a message: '*There is a ditch ahead.*' But that man did not look up to the sky and hence did not read the message. He fell into the ditch. The clouds felt sorry and thought, 'We put in so much effort to create this message, but couldn't save this man from falling in the ditch. Perhaps we did not provide the guidance in time and that's why this mishap occurred.'

They soon saw another man and instantly wrote a message for him: '*The thing you are asking for in your prayers is lying right in front of you.*' However, this man too didn't see the message. A huge diamond was lying right in the middle of his path but he did not notice it. If only he had received the guidance being given to him and seen that diamond, he would have become wealthy and his prayer would have been fulfilled. The clouds were astounded. They were keenly observing each passerby, instantly writing messages according to their needs, and erasing them to write new ones. The message would appear in the sky for a moment and then make way for the next message. This was not an easy job, but no one was being benefitted by it. No man ever looked up at the message or took heed. The entire effort was going in vain. The clouds were dejected. They went back to God and complained, 'We are ready to help everyone, but who will teach them to look up? Who will tell them that all the help they need can be received from above, if only they understand this guidance?'

This is the basic problem with us. We are not ready to receive guidance from God. We are unable to get His messages nor can we imbibe those messages. When we all learn to receive guidance from God (Consciousness/Self/Shiva/Allah/Lord/Divinity/Nature), not only our problems but most of the problems of this world will be solved. And then the play on the stage of this world will go on in an ideal manner, just as the producer/director of this play (God) wants it to. In that case, who can be a better guide to us than God?

Master : *I have been ringing the doorbell for the last half an hour! Couldn't you hear it?*

Servant : *You are the boss. You can ring the bell as long as you want. What can I do about it?*

God : **Interpret the meaning hidden in words, don't get stuck in words.**

Chapter 2

The Guide: Why Only God?

The Need for a Guide in this World

It is often seen that people run to various priests and ascetics in their quest for spiritual guidance. They may get stuck with a variety of mantras or tantric rituals. But can these provide you the right guidance? No. Only God can give you the right guidance.

God has created this Earth. This is His home. We are mere guests in His house. If we face any problems in this house, then the only wise thing to do is to consult the landlord himself.

Man is given guidance through diverse mediums but the Source is just one and that Source is God. Other things or people are mere channels; only God can give us true guidance. But we mistake the channels to be the Source. We get water from a tap, but the tap is merely a channel. How much water can a tap give? What is its capacity? Nothing much can be said about that because the tap is not the source, it is just a channel. On the other hand, if you wish to take water directly from the ocean, you will find that even after meeting all your needs the water level remains the same. The Source has everything in abundance. We may get tired of taking from the Source, but the Source never gets tired of giving, because it is abundant.

Most people cannot distinguish between a channel and the Source. They become satisfied with the little knowledge they receive from a channel. They do not know that the Source is a storehouse of unlimited knowledge and wisdom, while a channel is just a medium that leads us to that storehouse.

Why do we need guidance?

When you visit a historical site, you employ the services of a guide. You need a guide because you do not know much about that place and its history. Anyone who is not familiar with the path needs guidance. The guide provides you all the facts and myths about that place. He relates the important events that have taken place and other specialties of this place. He tells you about the history and geography of that area in easy to understand terms. This guidance makes your trip successful. If you did not have a guide, it would have taken you a lot of time to collect all the relevant information. You would have had to read and consult many thick books to get the right knowledge.

Drawing parallels, we are God's guests in this world. We have not created this world. This is not our real or permanent home. Even though scientists today claim to know a lot about this universe, the truth is that they still have not been able to unravel so many mysteries of the human body and the cosmos. Whatever issues they have been able to resolve were resolved because some people tuned into God's guidance and followed it.

We need wisdom to live in this unfamiliar world. God has sent us to this world on a special mission. What is this mission? What is the purpose of sending us to this planet? What is our role in this play of life on the stage of this world? We do not know any of this. We need God's help to know this.

Whether it is the stage of life or a movie, the director's role is crucial. The director alone tells you when and how to act under what circumstances. It may be a big banner film with the biggest star cast but the stars cannot do anything without a director. Just imagine, what will happen to a film which does not have a director? Each character will speak whatever dialogue he or she wishes to. No one will listen to anyone. That movie will be a flop show.

Similarly, you are an actor on the stage of life and God is the director of this play. He is continuously telling you about your role and its requirements. However, most people behave like clueless actors who don't know a thing about their respective roles. In that case, they need guidance. The director knows the entire story of the movie. He knows how every small dialogue too contributes to the total story. The actors' knowledge is limited while the director's knowledge is complete. That is why the actors listen to the director and follow his guidance. In the same way, we too must constantly take guidance from God and follow it.

Teacher (to a student who is very late for a class) : You are too early for the next class!

Student : My grandfather always says that arriving before time is a good habit.

God : Listen carefully before answering and don't try to act too smart.

Chapter 3

Seven Obstacles In Receiving Divine Guidance

Ask and It Shall be Given

If God is constantly guiding us, then why are we unable to receive this guidance? What are the obstacles? If we know these obstacles, it becomes easy to receive divine guidance. The seven main obstacles are:

First obstacle: Not being present at the right place

Supposing India and Australia are playing a one-day cricket match at Mumbai, but you go to Delhi to watch it. What will happen? You won't be able to watch the game. The game is being played, the players are playing, you have a ticket, but you cannot watch it because you are not at the right place.

Similarly, if we are to receive God's message at a specific place but if we are not present there, we won't receive the message.

Now the question arises, which is the right place for receiving God's guidance? Can this guidance be received only at holy places like Kaaba and Kashi? No! The right place is not a physical place; it is an inner place. We need to be present at our centre, i.e. our *tejasthan** or heart, to receive divine

---

**Tejasthan: It literally means the Bright Place. It actually means that place where the Self is connected with the body; where the formless and the form unite; where the union (yog) takes place. It can be roughly considered to be in the area of the heart. At some places in the book, it has been loosely translated as the 'heart'.*

guidance. When we are present at the right place, we receive guidance with ease.

Second obstacle: Not being present at the right time

The second main obstacle in receiving divine guidance is your absence at the right time. Supposing you are a cricket player and your match is to be played at 10 o'clock in the morning. If you go to play at 2:00 pm, what will happen? You will not be allowed to participate in the game. You may be a great player, but you need to reach the venue on time in order to play the game.

Sometimes, man asks for something at an inappropriate time, but according to God's plan that thing cannot be given to him at that particular time, for his own highest good. It is like a 6-year-old asking his parents to teach him to drive a car. His parents won't be able to do that because the time is not right for this particular request. When the right time comes, they themselves will organize the right training for him. This is what God does.

Also, we need not tell God how to guide us; this is His job. He knows His job better than we do. God opens the right door at the right time. Trust Him. If you want a door to open but it does not, this indicates that it is time to remain silent for a while.

Third obstacle: Lack of time

Lack of time is a major obstacle in receiving guidance from God. In today's busy life, man keeps running from pillar to post. Even if his body is resting, his mind keeps jumping here and there. His thoughts run amok like wild horses. He does not savour silence. In his spare time, he sits in front of the television so that his mind remains engaged. He has no time to listen to God's channel of silence. He does not know that silence is the channel through which he can receive divine guidance.

Today's world has become so fast paced that no one has time to listen or understand anything. If you wish to receive divine guidance, you will have to halt, understand, contemplate and be present.

Fourth obstacle: Not being prepared to receive guidance

If you want clean drinking water, you will not store it in a dirty, soiled pot. You will clean the pot before filling it up. Likewise, a level of preparation is required before we can receive guidance from God. If our mind is hyperactive (*rajoguni**) or lethargic (*tamoguni***), we cannot receive divine guidance.

We need to cleanse our mind of impurities. We need to scrub it clean with the brush of faith. We need to wash it well with positive thoughts. This is the preparation that needs to be done by us in order to receive unprecedented guidance.

Also, we need to quiet the incessant chatter of our mind and overcome the whirlwind of our thoughts. If our mind is full of our own thoughts, how will it accommodate divine thoughts or guidance? Even if the guidance is given to us,

we won't be able to receive it if we remain stuck in our own thoughts.

Fifth obstacle: Not asking for guidance

What you ask from God in your prayers, is what you get. He certainly opens the door, provided you knock at it.

If you visit someone's house and keep standing outside the door without knocking at it, will someone open the door for you? Not likely. The same is true with God as well. If you don't knock at His door, how will He open it? You don't

---

**Rajoguni: The one who possesses the quality of passion, activity, restlessness, aggressiveness. Rajoguna is the second of the three qualities of matter. Rajasic thoughts are thoughts of action, passion, creation, etc.*

** *Tamoguni: The one who possesses the quality of sloth and dullness. Tamoguna is the first of the three qualities of matter. Tamasic thoughts are characterized by laziness, dullness and lack of movement.*

need to knock loudly or repeatedly; just one gentle tap is enough. The door will then open on its own. We feel scared to knock at God's door. We think that a great amount of effort may be required to get it opened. It is a big door and looks quite heavy. We find excuse after excuse to avoid opening it. But when no other option is left and we finally try to open this door, we find that there was no barrier whatsoever—the door was merely an illusion! As long as we continue to sit at the seashore thinking 'The ocean must be very deep…I may drown…there may be dangers lurking below…,' the ocean will seem scary. But once we plunge in, we realize that it is not as bad as we had thought. It was just our imagination, an illusion.

What is meant by receiving guidance? If you believe life to be tough, you will stop moving ahead. But if you muster some courage and start walking, you will find that even a dark tunnel brightens up. It looked scary from outside, but as soon as you stepped in, light appeared. With each step, your path went on getting progressively illuminated. In the end you realize that you have crossed the big tunnel with such ease. The path kept getting illuminated on its own at the right time. God always provides right guidance at the right time; all you have to do is ask.

Sixth obstacle: Contradictory thoughts

Your contradictory thoughts pose a hurdle in receiving

guidance. If a question arises in your mind, then ideally you should stop to listen to the answer. According to the Law of Attraction, as soon as a question arises, its answer gets attracted towards you. This is an infallible law; there are no exceptions. The problem is that we ask a question but don't wait for the answer. We immediately ask another question which cancels the first question. This creates a dilemma because both questions are contradictory to each other.

Similarly, we desire one thing at one moment and the opposite thing the next moment. Consequently, none of our desires

get fulfilled. Mother Nature waits patiently for us to arrive at a definite desire before providing appropriate guidance.

For instance, a person prays, 'I want to go to Delhi.' The next day his prayers say, 'I don't want to leave Mumbai.' These are contradictory prayers. Due to such prayers, he either does not reach his destination or gets delayed unnecessarily.

A man is sick of his wife. He prays, 'I wish I could get freedom from all the quarrels and fights at home; I wish my wife improves and there is peace in our family.' Then intermittently he gets the thought, 'I wish I could get a divorce from her. That will be good riddance.' The fact is that every thought is a prayer. And people entertain such contradictory thoughts. One day they pray for the wife to improve and the next day they think of divorce. As a result of this, nature cannot provide correct guidance to them. Their confusion, problems and fights go on escalating.

When man encounters failure, thanks to his contradictory prayers, he protests, 'Why did this happen in my life? Why didn't I get all that I should have got?' He begins to think, 'This has happened because of my neighbour/my brother/my boss/my wife/my husband. I could not attain my rightful place in life because of this person.' He searches for the causes of his failure outside of himself. He does not realize that there is no one else to be blamed for his failures, but he himself. His contradictory thoughts are hindering his success.

The day he is clear about what he wants, he will begin to receive all the necessary guidance. He will then start taking the right steps and one day he will suddenly find himself at his destination. He will be amazed at his achievements. He will exclaim that he simply has no idea how everything happened. In order to reach this exalted state, we must contemplate and find out the areas in which we are indulging in contradictory prayers.

Seventh obstacle: Man's ego

Man's ego is the greatest obstacle in receiving divine guidance.

His ego makes him believe that there is only one-and-a-half brain in this world. One is with him and the remaining half is distributed amongst all the other people inhabiting this planet. He believes that he is the smartest, wisest, the most handsome and the most wonderful person in the world. His ego deflects the guidance coming towards him.

In order to receive guidance, man must trust God's intelligence and not his own. He should not consider his own intelligence to be the ultimate. He should admit that his intelligence is limited while God's intelligence is unlimited. We all should always put God in the first place. We should place implicit faith in God that He will show us the right direction to make our efforts fruitful.

Father : *Why are you rubbing your head with a bulb?*

Son : *I am trying to enlighten myself.*

God : **Do not use shortcuts for learning the Truth.**

Chapter 4

Seven Ways to Prepare Ourselves For Receiving Divine Guidance

Divine Plan

God has created you and loves you. He wants the very best for you. When you live your life according to His wish, you learn the purpose of your coming to Earth and how to fulfil this purpose.

Your life is proceeding according to a Divine Plan made specifically for you, but you are not aware of this. That is why you stay stuck in the vicious cycle of problems and sufferings. On receiving the right guidance, you will recognize the primary cause of problems. You can then use these problems as stepping stones to make your life trouble-free. Then that vicious cycle will change into a happy cycle.

Come, let us understand the divine plan and learn seven ways to prepare ourselves for receiving divine guidance.

1. **Open your closed fists**

    In order to receive God's guidance, you need to behave like a seeker. You need to realize the need for guidance. You have to come out of the illusion of *'I know everything and I am the best.'* This attitude closes your hands into fists. These closed fists do not let you receive anything. If you want God's guidance, you must open your hands, so that God will know that you are asking for something. Pray with open hands.

2. **Clean the windshield of your life's car**

   Supposing you are driving your car on a winter night. All of a sudden, the frost completely covers your windscreen. What is the result? The windscreen becomes foggy and you lose visibility. The possibility of an accident looms large. You slow down your speed to the bare minimum. This spoils your journey. You can carry on smoothly and speedily only after cleaning the windscreen. This signifies that you need to keep the windscreen of your life's car clean amidst the fog of everyday living.

   What is this windscreen? It is nothing but your mind. If this screen is dirty or foggy, you will not be able to see the path of your life clearly. There will be difficulty in receiving divine guidance. You must practise meditation to clear this fog from your mind. In order to prepare yourself for receiving guidance, you have to learn to remain in silence. You need to meditate. It is difficult to receive guidance in a hurry. You need to become like a blank paper, only then God can write something on it. If there is no empty space on your paper, how will God write on it? If your mind is quiet, only then will it get ready to meditate and you can receive divine guidance.

3. **Read spiritual books**

   God does not provide guidance by writing letters to us. He does not put up signboards saying: '*This is the right path. Walk on it.*' He only gives signals to us. One of the ways in which these signals can come to us is from spiritual texts or inspirational books. When we cultivate the habit of reading regularly, God finds it easy to guide us.

   While reading such books, your eye may fall upon such words which may be the answer to your problems. This is one of the ways of providing divine guidance. Sometimes some words touch your heart because they reflect your life. If you are sensitive, you can understand these signs.

4. **Keep company with Truth**

    Always keep company of good people. Stay in tune with the Truth. God sends messages through different channels. Sometimes a message comes to you through a friend's counsel, or a spiritual guru's discourse, or even the lyrics of a song. Sometimes you find the solution to your problem while discussing it with someone. We need to discuss meaningful matters with well-meaning people. Guidance cannot reach us while indulging in gossip, criticism, judgment or complaints. Guidance cannot reach us in the company of negative people. Therefore, keep company of positive people and Truth seekers.

5. **Develop awareness**

    If you wish to receive divine guidance, you will need to maintain awareness. You have to remain alert regarding how God is sending His guidance to you—which book or which person is being used as a medium. When you are aware, you may receive guidance through dreams or through some person's words. Sometimes a so-called coincidence may show you the right path. At times a closed door may lead you to the right path. All these are God's ways of guiding you.

    God does not offer guidance only from outside, he offers guidance from within as well. Your inner voice is soft but full of wisdom. Be attentive towards this soft inner voice.

6. **Take guidance from every mistake**

    A company hired a new manager. He was very capable and hence the owner gave him the power to take all decisions by himself. One day the manager committed a grave mistake, which cost the company millions of dollars. He wrote his resignation letter and submitting it to the owner said, 'I have caused a great loss to this company, hence I must leave.' The owner tore up the resignation letter and replied, 'The company has spent millions of dollars to help you learn this lesson; now you wish to go away with your learning from this incident! How can I let you go? You must stay here, because the lesson that you have learnt from this mistake will pay huge dividends in the future. I can't let you leave with such a valuable lesson.' The manager's morale was boosted seeing his superior's confidence in him. He stayed back, worked hard and earned manifold profits for his company.

Each mistake teaches you a lesson, but you don't learn that lesson unless you admit that you have committed the mistake. As long as you keep blaming others, you do not learn the lesson. As a result, you keep repeating the same mistake again and again. Nature wishes to teach you that lesson and that is why it keeps creating similar circumstances time and again. Until you learn the lesson, your circumstances won't change. When you admit your mistake and take guidance from nature, the same circumstances will not arise in the future.

7. **Look at the past to get guidance for the future**

    Contemplate and analyze past events. Reflect on what had happened in similar past circumstances. Analyze your current situation on the basis of your past experience. People who invest in the market look at the past charts to predict future possibilities. Big investors know that history repeats itself. You too need to take help from your past and develop awareness in order to receive guidance for your future. Do not undertake anything without giving due thought to it.

    If you analyze your past, you get the right guidance for the present. It means that whenever a problem arises, just analyze what had happened earlier under similar circumstances. Supposing you had taken a particular action and the result was not satisfactory, it means that you should not repeat it. On the other hand, you had taken another action and were successful in that situation, it means that you should repeat it.

It is not necessary to learn only from our own past experiences; if we are observant we can learn from others' experiences as well.

Patient : *Doctor, wherever I look, I see double of everything.*

Doctor : *Are all four of you suffering from this disease?*

God : **A doctor should heal himself first or heal himself in parallel while treating others.**

Chapter 5

Seven Steps of Guidance

First step: Form a relationship with God

The most important thing that you need to understand is: how to help God so that he can help you? There are seven steps for this. At the first step, you discover yourself by cultivating a relationship with God. God is guiding you. So, how are you taking it? How are you imbibing it? What is your relationship with God?

Think of God as a shopkeeper and you as a customer. In other words, He is the giver and you are a receiver. While making your purchases, you should not bargain with God. When we are filled with ego, we are not in a receptive mode. We declare, 'Let these particular things happen. Only then will I believe in God, otherwise not.' We should give God what he wants. God wants only two things from us—faith and love. What's interesting is that both are already present inside us; albeit in a latent state. Miracles happen when faith and love are awakened.

Making an arduous journey, people reach temples situated upon hills and mountains. Their faith is awakened on completing the difficult journey and hence they get results. Faith is already present inside them, only it has not manifested or released from the confines of their minds. Some films don't get released and remain canned. They serve no purpose. Is our faith and love canned as well? We need to open these cans and release these precious feelings so as to allow them to manifest.

We do not understand God's guidance in our ignorance. God is guiding us at each step, every day, in each event, and for every problem; but we cannot receive this guidance if we have not become a receiver.

Various forms of our body

Our body takes on various forms throughout the day. It receives various things in accordance with its forms. Of course we must remember that we are not the body; we are only operating through this body.

As mentioned earlier, our body changes forms many times during a day. When we eat, our body becomes a dining room. When we sleep, it becomes a bedroom. When we go to school or college, it becomes a classroom. When we watch television, it becomes a theatre. And when we are in the office, it acts like a cabin. Thus, our body functions in different ways at different places. When we sit in meditation, it becomes a meditation room. When we are in *satsang* it becomes a place of worship. *(Sanskrit, sat = ultimate truth, sang = company. Thus, satsang means the company of the ultimate truth.)* In this form, the body is most receptive for divine guidance.

To enable us to receive divine guidance, the body turns us sometimes into Mr. Ears, sometimes into Ms. Eyes and sometimes into Dr. Feelings.

Mr. Ears — Guidance through the inner ear

Some people (irrespective of gender) receive guidance through listening. Their mind's prattle goes on but they receive divine guidance intermittently. Such people are more tuned to spoken words. These words are not sounds they can hear externally; rather it means that they can hear

God's voice from within them. You too may have noticed that a never-ending train of thoughts begins as soon as you wake up in the morning, but suddenly a voice from within calls out to you, 'Do this; this will be better for you.' If you listen to this voice and obey it, you achieve success. This was God's voice and you are Mr. Ears. People who recognize such signals end up doing the toughest tasks with ease. They are praised by everyone. However, if they don't take the credit for it and remain with an attitude of gratitude, the possibility of receiving further guidance increases manifold.

Thus, Mr. Ears receives guidance through the internal ear.

Ms. Eyes — Guidance through visuals

Some people (irrespective of gender) receive guidance through visuals. They may be engaged in some project and suddenly some images flash in their minds. They then work according to those images and accomplish their project successfully. This visual guidance comes straight from the Source. Such people's memory is also visual and they cannot grasp words as much as pictures. For example, a person is preparing a model for building something. Suddenly, the entire finished picture flashes before his eyes. He works according to that picture and succeeds. He does not know the source of the visual; but his being immersed in his work is an indication to nature that he is ready for it. When you go to sleep at night, you don't say, 'I will go to bed only when I feel sleepy.' You go and lie down on your bed when it's time to sleep. When you show your readiness, sleep comes automatically. It is important to show your readiness first.

Some people get guidance through dreams. There is an incident which dates back to the period when the needle was not yet invented. Sewing clothes was a tough task. People used to make holes into the cloth material with a sharp object and then pass a thread through those holes. It was a tedious and laborious job. There was a man who used to wonder as

to what should be done so that the thread could pass along with the sharp object through the material. Suddenly one night he had a dream in which he saw a field of sugarcanes. The sugarcanes looked somewhat different. He looked closely and noticed that each sugarcane had a hole at one end. This image inspired him to make a sharp object with a hole at one end. Thus, the needle was invented.

Some faculties are active or predominating in each body according to the constitution of the body and also according to the individual's level of readiness. In some people, Mr. Ears is predominant, in some Ms. Eyes and in some Dr. Feelings.

Dr. Feelings — Guidance through feelings

Dr. Feelings are those people (irrespective of whether they are doctors or not) who receive guidance through a certain feeling or vibration in their body. When they set out to do something good, they experience a special vibration. They cannot catch words, nor do they see any images. They receive guidance through feelings from within. For instance, you meet someone and the vibration, vibe or feeling inside you, tells you that he is a good man. You do not know this man but you get tuned with him. You listen to a quote and you get the feeling, 'Yes! This is for me.' Why? If you can't grasp or explain that in words, you are Dr. Feelings. The prefix *Dr.* has been added because these bodies easily grasp others' vibes or feelings too. Such people make highly successful nurses and doctors.

If interviewers can get such vibes, their task will become simple. Thousands of candidates appear for various interviews. The right candidates have to be chosen after intensive questioning. In such a situation, a Dr. Feeling can make the correct choices based upon his feeling.

Now you have think on: how do you receive guidance? Are you Mr. Ears, Ms. Eyes or Dr. Feelings? It is possible that some of you may have two simultaneous traits. One trait may be predominant and the other may also be present. Someone may be Mr. Eyes, but his Ms. Eyes faculty too may be gradually gaining strength. In any case, one trait is always more dominant than the other. It is important to recognize the category you belong to, in order to understand how nature guides you.

Employer : Have you watered the plants today?

Servant : No Sir, it is raining outside.

Employer : You lazy bum! Go, take an umbrella and do your job.

God   : Throw the umbrella and wake up.

Chapter 6

Second Step: Whatever You Do, Do It With A Smile

Create a positive and happy environment

The second step to help God to help us is: Whatever you do, do it with a smile. When you smile and do things, you automatically feel happy and also create a positive and happy environment around you. Additionally, it is easier for you to manifest love and faith for all when you are happy. By smiling you are indicating: 'Dear God, whatever you are doing for me is just right for me. My smile expresses my faith in You and in others too. It tells everyone that I love and trust them.'

A father tells his little son, 'I will buy you a bicycle tomorrow.' The boy starts jumping with joy and happily goes to sleep that night with dreams of the bicycle he is going to ride tomorrow. He has no such doubt as to whether his father will really buy him the bicycle or not. We too need to trust God with such child-like faith. Through all the holy scriptures, God gives us the message: 'There is abundance of love, joy, health, wealth, courage and all the other good things on Earth. There is no lack or deficiency whatsoever.' Even after this assurance, if we do not trust God, then it is our fault. The right way of arousing our latent faith is by doing everything happily with a smile.

'Whatever you do, do it with a smile' also means that we should do everything like a swan. According to the scriptures, swans are known to pick up only pearls among all things. Similarly, we too must pick up only the pearls of wisdom among the many kinds of things that we encounter in our everyday lives. We should not cry over trifles, or cheat others, or engage in any sort of deception or corruption. Instead we need to carry out noble deeds with joy and laughter so that our laughter touches the hearts of others and spreads joy among them.

Laughter is a crucial part of our lives. Laughter generates happiness. Our happiness has a pleasant effect not only on our internal environment but also on our external environment. However, people hardly laugh nowadays. Most of the time they are busy grumbling, criticizing others, or discussing their individual problems. Complaining and cribbing has become a part of our nature and we have forgotten to laugh. Joy and laughter is our basic nature but today we need a reason to laugh, otherwise we cannot laugh. That is why you see many people going to laughter clubs these days, where they learn to laugh with the help of fake laughter.

Happy thoughts beget happy events

When you stay happy throughout the day and thereby constantly express your love and faith, good things start happening in your life. You become a magnet and start attracting the best as per the law of attraction.

A happy person gets magnetized for good things, just like a philosopher's stone, and attracts positivity in his life. In contrast, an unhappy person attracts negativity. Joy magnetizes you for all the best things in the world. But you are not aware of what all can be achieved with this magnetism! What you can attract by being unhappy is evident in your life. Hence, start being happy consciously.

Whatever good exists in your life is because you have been somewhat happy at times. For instance, you enjoyed watching a good show on the television. You felt happy on meeting a dear one. You enjoyed during your brother's wedding. You laughed when you were with friends. You felt joy while patting your pet dog. These small happy moments also create something positive in your life.

Don't ever think that something good has happened with you because you yearned and whined for it. Don't be under the impression that someone felt pity for you and gave you what you wanted. In fact, good things have come into your life because of the joy you felt, no matter how little, during any little incidence. But, as we can't understand this truth, we start grumbling every now and then, and forget to laugh.

Now let us focus on laughter. Laughter is of four types. It is important to understand what kind of laughter we have at present and what kind we must actually have.

Four kinds of laughter

1. Lip laughter
2. Head laughter
3. Discriminative laughter
4. Heart laughter

Lip laughter

The first kind of laughter is limited to the lips only. This laughter does not originate from the heart; it is confined to the lips alone. This laughter is usually cynical. It indicates the pleasure people derive from teasing, hurting, mimicking, deriding, or cheating others.

Let us understand it through an example. A few friends were enjoying their meal with a curry made of eggplants. One of them said, 'Anyone who eats eggplants becomes a donkey in his next life.' The other friend quipped at once, 'Is that so? But now this knowledge is of no use to you. You should have thought of that in your previous birth.' You see what happened here? One friend tried to tease the other, but the other one was smarter. When people do not know real laughter, they take recourse to such cheap thrills.

Head laughter

The second kind of laughter is the head laughter or intelligent laughter. This laughter is one step higher than lip laughter. Here you do not tease someone to laugh. Instead, you use your intelligence to laugh. Let's understand this through an example. There was a billboard on a highway that read: *Those who were in a hurry, have already departed!* This is intelligent humour. The statement beautifully conveyed that accidents occur when you drive at high speed and those who were driving in a hurry have already departed from this world; therefore please slow down. If a person reads this and uses his intellect, he will laugh.

Discriminative laughter

When the intellect is pure and has gained a certain depth and wisdom, the joy of discriminative intelligence (*vivek-anand*) arises. Discriminative Intelligence means the intelligence which can differentiate between the truth and falsehood. Once you have learnt the secrets of life, you can face any situation with awareness. Your main focus remains upon the Ultimate Truth under all circumstances. You learn the secret of death and understand the reality of suffering. When the joy of discrimination arises, your laughter becomes discriminative.

Heart laughter

When a thought appears after taking a dip in the heart, you have a heart laugh. Mental thoughts cannot bring such joy, because the mind buzzes with thoughts, while the heart contains deep inner silence or *moun*. When thoughts enter this silence, real laughter emerges. Real laughter arises when you recognize your true self, i.e. after self-realization. All thoughts arise from your heart or tejasthan after self-realization. This is silent bliss. This state is a step higher than discriminative laughter.

Raise the level of your laughter

Having understood the four types or levels of laughter, you need to find out what is your level. Your eyes clearly indicate

whether your laughter is from your lips, your intellect, your viveka, or from your heart. Your eyes are the windows of your internal state. They disclose the level of your laughter. Learn how to create an atmosphere of smiles and laughter. Your goal is to awaken and fully manifest the love and faith from your heart so that your laughter is from your heart. If you find it difficult to reach the level of heart laughter, you must aim to reach at least the level of discriminative laughter. Don't get stuck in lip laughter. Move ahead, even if it is one step at a time.

Learn to laugh at yourself

Laughing at others is the lowest form of laughter. It is the most harmful and negative level. It is essential to rise above this level. If you must laugh at someone, learn to laugh at yourself. Learn to laugh at your mistakes. Laughing at yourself will take you to your heart. When you refuse to accept and laugh at your mistakes, you remain stuck in your head and block your growth. Therefore, it is important to learn to laugh at your mistakes. Bigger the mistake, louder the laugh. Man's biggest mistake is that he considers himself to be the body. Laugh out loud at this mistake!

If a swan is coloured black and starts crowing thinking itself to be a crow, isn't that a big mistake? The day it understands its mistake, its laughter arises from the heart. That day it becomes a *paramhansa*. (*Paramhansa means the supreme swan and this term is used for a self-realized master. A swan feels at home on both land and water. Similarly, a true sage is equally at home both in the materialistic world [realms of matter] and in silence. Also, the swan, according to Indian scriptures, is able to separate milk from water. Thus, the swan symbolizes the ability of a self-realized master to separate Truth from delusion.*) The *paramhansa* laughs at itself and says, 'How did I think I was a crow! It was just a belief and now it's gone.' In the same way, man considers himself to be the body. The more he becomes aware of this mistake, the easier it is for him to receive guidance.

Whatever you do, do it with a smile

Whatever you do, you must be happy while doing it. When you laugh, your celebration is not just for that moment alone. Your laughter tells God, 'Dear God, I am happy in your will. Your will is my will. I have complete faith that whatever You do for me is for my highest good.' Your laughter is your *faith in action*.

God has been giving you everything in His own way, through His own channels. All you have to do is, do everything with a smile and keep raising the level of your laughter to make it a heart laughter. This is a powerful way to indicate your faith and receive guidance from God.

Family's mission statement

In our family, we must help each other remember the mantra: 'Whatever you do, do it with a smile.' Make this your family's mission statement. All your family members can get together for a meeting and decide about the kind of home environment they want to live in and how everyone can work towards it. They can decide to share all the household chores with a smile. The day you have guests at home, you should definitely decide to apply the mantra. When you follow the mantra, the children in your family will learn it as well. In fact, they are the ones who will remind you to smile if you forget. When you get upset, stressed, worried or sad, they will repeat, 'Whatever you do, do it with a smile.' If you don't wish to say the whole sentence every time, you can use a pre-determined hand gesture instead. That way the message gets easily communicated.

If the other person is crying, you can show the hand gesture as a reminder. Even then if she does not understand, show her a joker's cap or a cartoon. Decide in advance what sign you will use in your family to help others remember this mission statement.

There is no doubt that the whole family will agree to this mantra. Everyone wants love, trust and happiness in the family. If such an atmosphere of joy has not been created in your home, it only means that you have not made a decision to achieve it; you have not made it your aim. All family members must sit together and decide the principles they will follow for their home. When all agree to them, there can be so much love and joy in the family that all doors of guidance will open up. The help that God wishes to send to you will reach you effortlessly.

Teacher : *You can't sleep in my class!*

Student : *If you speak softly, I can.*

God : **It is easy to remain unconscious. Consciousness is difficult but essential.**

Chapter 7

Third Step: Unlocking

Develop and maintain good relations with people

The third step is that of unlocking. We need to unlock all the channels through which God sends guidance to us. That way, we can help God in helping us faster.

When all the taps in your house are closed, you won't know whether water supply from the main tank has started or not. You need to have at least one tap open. Likewise, you will not know if God's guidance has arrived unless your channels are open.

Supposing God wants to send you a message or a gift. Then how will He send it? He will send it through some person. But if you have had a fight with that particular person, how will you receive it? God finds it very difficult to send gifts to people who quarrel with everyone, because He cannot find any delivery channels for them.

Maintaining good relationships with everyone will facilitate in receiving help from God. This does not mean that you need to socialize excessively. But at least you should not stop talking to people. Many a time people stop speaking to each other for as long as 10-20 years due to some difference of opinions. Thus, they end up closing many channels of guidance. Check if you too have closed most of your channels; if so it is time to open them now.

People readily share with you any important information they have received if you have a good relationship with them. They will text you, call you, or visit you to offer help only when you are on good terms with them; not otherwise. God too conveys information meant for you through someone with whom you have cordial relations so that you get the information. But if you have hardly any good relations, all messages and gifts will take a long route to reach you. Hence, keep your channels open to receive a speedy delivery from God.

If you have been having clashes with everyone, then the information may reach right next door, but it won't reach you! Supposing you want a special book which is not available in India but is available in the U.S. Incidentally, your neighbour is a bookseller who can place an order for this book. But the problem is that you had recently had an argument with him and are consequently not on good terms with him. Under such circumstances, you will hesitate in taking his help to order the book. And, even if you ask him, he will not oblige you because of the grudge. Fortunately, another neighbour's cousin stays in the U.S., and he can get this book for you, but you have had a dispute with him as well. Yet another neighbour already owns this book but you had a major tussle with him just last month. In such a situation, none of them will help you, nor will you ask for their help.

The above example illustrates the point that spoiling your relations with everyone around will close all avenues of help. Thereby you create hurdles and delay the fulfilment of your own desires. Understand the direct connection between the two. The clearer the channels, the sooner are your desires fulfilled. God needs some medium to send you what you need. Thus, anyone with harmonious relationships easily gets what he wants because his channels are open.

Some people often complain, 'Why don't we get any information?' They get angry at this but never stop to ask themselves, 'What if I am at fault? Perhaps I am responsible for the information not reaching me. Is there any block in my thought process? Is there any block in my relationships?'

A pebble in the water pipe can block the water flow. Only when all the pebbles are removed will the water flow freely to you. This implies that only when you remove all the blocks from your life, the guidance from God will reach you at the earliest.

The sun is shining bright in the sky, but if the sunlight is not reaching your room, it only means that the doors and windows of your room are closed. Open the doors and windows of your life to receive divine light. If you cannot unlock them, divine guidance will fail to reach you. So, what is the password to unlock them? The password is: *Whatever you do, do it with a smile.* When you live in joy, your relationships will go on improving. Additionally, you will feel good in the company of others.

Points to remember while dealing with people:

1. Use your head for yourself and your heart for others

Whenever you deal with people, use your heart; and whenever you deal with yourself, use your head. But almost always we do just the opposite. We use the heart for ourselves and say, 'I am such a good person. I committed this mistake, but there's a reason behind it.' We are liberal and compassionate with ourselves, nevertheless if the same mistake is committed by anyone else, we don't spare that poor fellow. There we use our head. Actually, it should be the other way round.

2. Look at your actions and others' intentions

Again, we do just the opposite. We consider our intentions and support our actions. We think, 'Even if I hurled some abuses at my neighbour, it's alright because my intention was good… I want him to improve.' But when someone abuses us, we get furious as we look only at his action and overlook his intention. Basically, we should pay attention to the intention behind anybody's behaviour. However, the reverse happens. We don't make the slightest effort to ask, 'Why did you do this? What was your intention? Did you wish to hurt

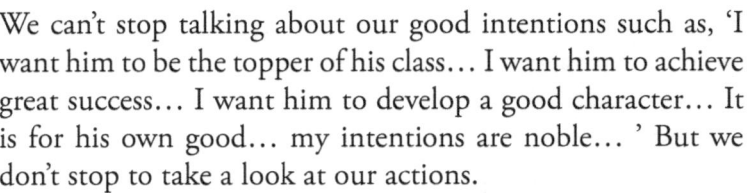

me?' If you had asked, the answer would have most probably been, 'No, that was not my intention.'

We can't stop talking about our good intentions such as, 'I want him to be the topper of his class… I want him to achieve great success… I want him to develop a good character… It is for his own good… my intentions are noble… ' But we don't stop to take a look at our actions.

When we stop and think for a while, the knots in our relationships start opening and the walls of separation begin to crumble. Uptil now we have been looking at our intentions and others' actions, hence we kept boasting of our goodness. But from now onwards, let's pay attention to our actions and others' intentions.

3. Be hard on yourself and soft on others

We always treat ourselves with kid gloves. This means that when we commit a mistake it is always unintentional, but if others do the same it is always intentional, and we immediately pounce upon them. We don't even pause for a moment to think why he would have done that. We need to choose the middle path, neither hard nor soft. In fact, we should actually be hard on ourselves and soft on others.

When we use our intellect, we will understand that we should not be too liberal with ourselves as that can impede our growth. Whatever we have done till now can be excused, nonetheless from now on we need to be firm. This does not mean that we should not love ourselves. We must love ourselves but also make ourselves work to grow and progress. We must pamper ourselves but not to an extent that it may hamper our growth. We need to eliminate all those patterns and wrong habits that create an obstruction in our growth path.

Even a small pattern can become a hurdle and stop your progress. Hence, clear your blocks and make sure that all your channels are open. When people feel good talking to you and their consciousness level rises on interacting with you, it means that there is a free flow between you and God. Consequently, God's message will reach you very fast.

At this step, it is important to understand people's feelings in order to realize their intentions and develop good relations with them. Become Dr. Feelings.

4. First understand people and then try to improve them

A king sent his son for his formal education at a guru's ashram. When his education was over, the king went to fetch him. On seeing the king approaching them, the guru started beating the prince black and blue. The king was enraged and thought, 'Why is he beating him so badly, without any apparent reason?' In those days, a guru was always highly revered, and so the king did not utter a word but he couldn't stop his turbulent thoughts. He quietly watched his son getting beaten up and the prince too silently bore the brunt of his master's stick. When the master was done and threw the stick aside, the king couldn't hold himself any longer and asked, 'Venerable Guruji, why did you beat him?' The guru replied, 'My dear king, this was his last lesson. His education is now complete. One day he too will become the king and one of his duties will be to punish the guilty. However, he should know what is pain and suffering so that he is sensitive while deciding the punishment. Today's lesson has taught him just that.'

We can unlock vibrant relationships only when we understand each other's feelings. And then God can easily send his guidance to us.

Boy   : *Why do you wear these glasses? You look like an owl in them.*

Friend : *I am helpless. If I don't wear these glasses, you look like an owl to me!*

God   : Don't look for owls; look for swans.

Chapter 8

Fourth Step: Become Newton And Learn Something New

Flexibility and Change

At the fourth step, you need to learn something new. You have to take a new turn and you have to become Newton, the famous scientist. This means you need to conduct new experiments like him. As soon as Newton saw an apple falling from a tree, he decoded the message and discovered the Law of Gravity. Nature sends messages to everyone but not all can decode them. This is because they don't know how to interpret them. Thousands of people must have seen apples falling from trees before Newton, but they could not decode the message. Newton had an open and flexible mind, that's the reason he could easily interpret the message. To become open and flexible, we need to take a new turn and become Newton.

Rigidity — an obstacle in conducting new experiments

Rigid people neither want to hear anything new, nor do they want to try new experiments. They don't want to give up their age-old beliefs and prefer to remain satisfied with what they have. They do not want to progress. Though they can see that the world has advanced and drastically changed, yet they want to carry on with their old ways. Thus, rigid people close the doors of opportunity and growth for themselves, while flexible people are able to grasp and implement new guidance.

In the cricket ground, a flexible fielder can bend, jump or twist his body to swiftly catch the ball. If a fielder's body is not flexible, he can hurt himself. Scared of spraining or straining his muscles, he does not even try to bend or twist and hence the catch slips past him. In the same way, all divine signals slip past an inflexible individual. A flexible person, when hungry, starts eating irrespective of how the food is being served and who is serving it. On the contrary, a rigid person says, 'I like to eat food only in my own plate. Serve it in my plate and my bowl.' He is adamant and expects to be served the food he likes and in the way he likes. As a result, he is left hungry. He thus acts against his own interests.

Be flexible

Being flexible means adapting yourself to the existing circumstances. If you continue to cling to your ideas, you will not be able to take what is being offered. This is similar to a beggar who refuses to take pennies in alms because he thinks that receiving anything less than a dollar is below his dignity! If he analyzes his situation, he will realize that a beggar is dependent upon others' mercy. He should gratefully accept whatever is being given to him, otherwise he won't get anything.

When Newton saw an apple falling from a tree, a thought popped up in his mind: 'Why didn't the apple go up? Why did it come down?' Although countless people before him had witnessed falling apples, but this thought did not arise in any of them, because they were rigid. They did not question their belief that things always fall down.

If you don't ask a question, you won't receive an answer

Newton asked a question and discovered the law of gravity. How will we get an answer if we don't ask a question? How will we make new discoveries? Asking questions increases our flexibility. For a long time, *Doordarshan* was the only television channel in India. Its programs were informative but not very interesting. Yet people continued to watch them and did nothing about it, until one entrepreneur asked himself, 'Why can't I start a private TV channel?' He pursued the answer to its logical conclusion despite all the challenges and bureaucratic red tape he had to encounter in the process. Soon he started his own private channel and the rest is history. Similarly, another man asked, 'Why can't a car cost just one lakh rupees?' He made such a car and changed the history and economics of car production. These real-life examples prove that you will receive answers only when you ask questions. If you remain stuck in old beliefs and patterns, you won't create anything new. If in the future too you will keep doing what you are doing in the present, you will keep getting the same as what you have got in the present. If you want something new, you have to do something new.

Flexibility — a sign of receptivity

Mother Nature is constantly guiding us, but we need to develop mental flexibility in order to understand this guidance. Our tongue is flexible, while our teeth are hard. Most often teeth break in old age, while the tongue works just fine throughout life. Flexibility of the tongue is a boon in itself because of which it remains safe even between a set of hard teeth.

Thus, if you wish to learn the art of receiving guidance from nature, you will need to be open and flexible. Plants, trees, flowers, leaves, the wind, the sky, the moon and stars are conveying some messages to us at all times. When we sit in meditation with them, we will get many insights. Mother Nature and God Father are our real parents and they are constantly communicating with us and guiding us. The only thing is we have to learn to take guidance from them.

People live in the same old manner all their lives. They spend their day in the same way as they have for years together. They wake up in the morning, have tea, breakfast, get ready and leave for work. Then they come back from office, watch television, have dinner and go to sleep. If someone tells them about a new way of living life, they say, 'We don't have time.' They do not change their ways, hence everything remains the same for them.

It's time to take a new step, a new turn. When you take a new turn, many new secrets of God's guidance will be revealed to you, just like it happened with Newton.

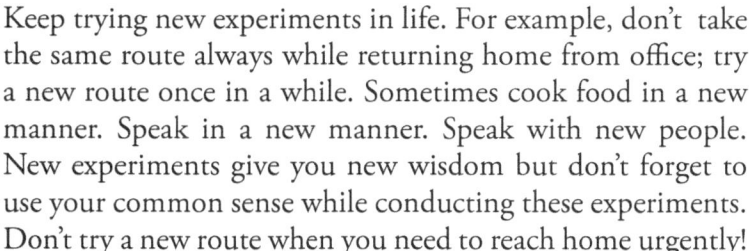

Keep trying new experiments in life. For example, don't take the same route always while returning home from office; try a new route once in a while. Sometimes cook food in a new manner. Speak in a new manner. Speak with new people. New experiments give you new wisdom but don't forget to use your common sense while conducting these experiments. Don't try a new route when you need to reach home urgently!

If no one ever did anything new in this world, we would have still been travelling by the bullock cart and working only in the fields. There would have been no industry and no electricity; the phone and the internet would be simply out of question. There would have been no hospitals, nor any banks. We would have still been taking loans from money-lenders and getting treatment from quacks. Human beings have been progressing because of indulging in new activities. The Self, God or Consciousness within us enjoys new experiences through each one of us. Experiences of the older generation benefit the new generation. That's why children of the new generation are always smarter than children of the older generation. You may also have observed that the new generation is always more advanced, more modern and more open in their outlook of life.

Change — a sign of progress

You may face many obstacles while doing something new; such as people may criticize you or you may lose self-confidence. Ordinary people prefer the status quo. They resist new thoughts and are content with their old beliefs. That is the reason why every new thought is first opposed. Any person who undertakes to do something new must remember that people are generally conventional in their outlook, but only change can bring progress. When Galileo said that the Earth revolves around the Sun, he was condemned and tortured. People of that time believed that the Sun revolved around the Earth. Galileo had spoken the truth but his truth was against the prevalent belief, and so he had to bear the consequences.

Today, history commends his courage for discovering and disseminating the truth. It is not easy to do something new. It requires will power and the courage of conviction. It needs audacity to withstand the arrows of criticism. Critics look at the past, while a man of new thought looks at the possibilities of the future.

Stay ready to face resistance to your new ideas. Not only your enemies but also your friends will oppose. Your enemies will oppose you because of their enmity. They don't want you to progress. On the other hand, your well-wishers will oppose you because they fear that you may fail or harm yourself. They look at the risks, not at the possibilities. They look at the difficulties, not at the growth. They look at the darkness, not at the light!

Divine help — at the right time

Supposing a great thought flashes in your mind and you start working upon it. However, the moment you encounter a hurdle, you get anxious and start thinking, 'Perhaps this is not the right idea, maybe this formula won't work, what if I am not capable enough to accomplish this task...' Please remember at such times that if a thought has appeared in your mind due to divine guidance, then you will also be given the right tools for its completion by the divine. Have complete faith in Him. Before leaving your house don't try to ensure that all the traffic signals along the way should be green. Just have faith that as soon as you reach a traffic signal, God will turn it into green. You will receive the right tools at the right time, automatically. If God has given you the guidance to undertake something new, He will also make all the required arrangements and ensure its completion. Your job is to just become a channel through which the divine guidance can flow and materialize. If you won't do this job, God will guide someone else and get it done. Simply trust that when the time comes, God will give you the strength to complete the job.

Let us understand this through an example taken from the life of Thomas Edison. Edison has many inventions to his name, including that of the light bulb. It is a fact that whenever an idea of a new invention emerged in his mind due to divine guidance, he would call a press conference and announce the completion date of the project. He would then get busy with his experiments to keep up with the deadline. He would invariably come up with the invention by the proclaimed date. This means that people who have complete faith in God's guidance must break all the back-bridges and trust that all the required resources will be provided and the task will be completed successfully.

New activity, new experience

Think about how you have progressed from your childhood till now. What would have happened if you had not done anything new? You would have still been sleeping in a crib and drinking milk from a bottle. But you kept learning and doing new things. You learnt how to crawl, walk, run, and jump. Then you learnt to speak. You first learnt your mother tongue and later moved on to other languages. You practised until you became proficient in them. This is how man progresses. He does something new and learns something new from it. If he had not learnt any new activities, he would have been living in the jungles even now. God experiences this world with the help of man. He keeps providing new opportunities to man so that He can keep getting new experiences.

Do not misuse your knowledge

Doing new experiments does not mean trying alcohol, drugs or the like. A new task is not just any new task. It implies those new actions which are in accordance with divine guidance. And the divine does not guide anyone to do anything wrong. We must turn our mental antenna in the right direction and only then we can catch the right signals.

Policeman: Aren't you ashamed of stealing a hundred rupee note from my wallet?

Wife   : Why are creating such a racket? Take these fifty rupees and close the case right here.

God   : Don't be a slave of wrong habits.

Chapter 9

Fifth Step: Awaken the Wise Inner Voice

Pay attention to divine feedback

Faith in God implies that even though you don't know where God is taking you, yet you are willing to be led by Him because you love Him and trust Him. You know that wherever He is taking you, it is the best for you.

When you have been working according to His guidance for a long time, you will notice something strange. You will gradually find that you are not being given as much guidance as before. It's nothing to be worried about. The reason is that you have automatically started doing everything in the right manner! When children are young, you have to guide them time and again. With the right training, they take right decisions on their own when they grow up. The same thing happens with divine guidance. You need more guidance while moving from darkness to light. Once you are in the light, the guidance is no longer required.

Listen to your inner voice

At the fifth step to help God to help us, we need to listen to our inner voice in order to receive divine guidance. This little voice speaks to us through our intuition. Just as a teacher gives tuition, God too gives us tuition through intuition. We must learn to gain wisdom through this medium too.

Mother Nature guides us through external channels, while

God Father guides us from within through intuition. You don't have to wander around to seek wisdom. You don't have to pursue any saint or sage. You don't have to use tantras or mantras. God has made arrangements for you to receive wisdom from within. Even so, we needlessly go from pillar to post in search of Truth. Little are we aware that the Truth lies right within us. This is just like a musk deer that carries the musk pod in its belly but keeps searching everywhere for the source of the enigmatic fragrance.

> Socrates was a great philosopher in ancient Greece. Once a young man approached him and expressed his desire to attain wisdom. Socrates took him to the riverbank and asked him to get into the water with him. Both got into the water. Suddenly, Socrates caught hold of the youth's neck and put his head under water. Initially, the young man thought it was a joke, but when he couldn't breathe anymore he started struggling. Yet Socrates did not let go. At last, the young man tried with all his might and managed to get his head out of the water. Coughing up a lot of water, he cried, 'Have you gone crazy? I asked you how to attain wisdom, not how to court death!' Socrates smiled and stated, 'When you struggle for wisdom as much as you were struggling for breath, you will automatically receive it.'

The above snippet clearly illustrates that wisdom is easily available. The problem is not with the availability of wisdom, the problem lies with our intention to receive it. We don't desire wisdom so bad that it becomes a matter of life and death. Remember the law of attraction? Whenever you have an intense desire for something, it gets attracted towards you. If you have a strong desire for guidance, and you keep thinking about it all the time, you will definitely receive it. However, what usually happens is that you think about guidance for about a few minutes today and then you think about it again after a month! If your desire is so weak, how can you receive divine guidance? Make your desire so strong that your inner voice can reach you.

The inner voice is very soft. It's not easy to hear it. In contrast, our mind keeps buzzing with loud thoughts all the time that are difficult to ignore. Hence, we need to make an effort and sit in meditation to stop the mind's buzz, because only then are we able to hear the little inner voice. This can be achieved with training and practice. The good news is once this dialogue begins, it will continue. You start receiving guidance from within and experience great joy.

Practise listening to the inner voice

If you are alert, you will be able to grasp every small intuition you receive. Then you won't need anyone else to answer your questions. You can just ask yourself and get the answer from within. You can begin with an experiment. Whenever your phone rings, ask yourself, 'Whose call can it be?' Then wait for a second to hear the answer from within and then answer the phone. Thereafter, you will notice that usually your first guess is correct. However, if you start thinking logically, 'It is 6 o' clock now, therefore this particular person must be calling,' then the answer has come from your brain and not from your intuition. Logic is based upon the intellect, whereas the inner voice or intuition is based on the Truth within.

You will need practice to strengthen your intuition. Whenever your doorbell rings, ask yourself who could it

be and listen to the answer from within. Then you can open the door. You can make it a game and try it every time. At first you may get wrong answers, yet continue with it. Don't worry whether your first guess is right or wrong. Don't get stuck in right or wrong. Just learn to ask. Ask and you shall receive. Only those who have asked have received.

Initially seek guidance on smaller things

Start by seeking guidance for smaller issues. When you become an expert at this with regular practice, you can then confidently seek guidance for major decisions. Trust your intuition, but also keep analyzing it. Keep a count of your validated intuitions. When the number of right intuitions starts rising, it means that you are becoming an expert at it. Nevertheless, do not take big decisions based upon your intuition at the beginning itself. For example, don't decide immediately to change your job saying that you were guided by your intuition. Move slowly. Climb one step at a time. Don't try to reach the top in one leap.

When listening to your intuition, remember that the first thought or first gut feeling is generally right. Then again, there is an exception to this rule. If your first thought is negative, then the second thought is right. Understand the difference. When you are doing something positive, then your first thought is right. When you are doing something negative, then your second thought is right. Supposing, your first thought is, 'Let me curse this person right now,' then immediately look for the second thought. The second thought says, 'I will curse him after two days.' This is the right thought. Go with it.

If you are stuck with your inherited habits, it means that you are not yet free. If your mom was terrified of lizards and so are you, then it is obvious that you have not attained freedom. We must listen to our real parents—Mother Nature and God Father. We must get tuned with them. We must develop the habit of asking questions to ourselves and listening to our inner voice.

Pay attention to the body's feedback

Our body gives feedback for each and every thing. For instance, if our body needs water, we feel thirsty. If it needs energy, we feel hungry. If we keep awake late into the night, our eyes start burning. If we don't exercise our body, we feel lazy. In the same manner, our body-mind mechanism gives feedback through feelings too. Whenever we do something good for others, we experience a feeling of satisfaction. A sad event evokes the feeling of sorrow. When our ego is hurt, we feel angry. When someone praises us, we feel happy. A feeling of devotion arises while praying. Understand this feedback of your feelings. Whenever a feeling arises, analyze it by asking, 'Why did this feeling arise?' If you are feeling angry, ask yourself, 'Has my ego been hurt in any way?' You

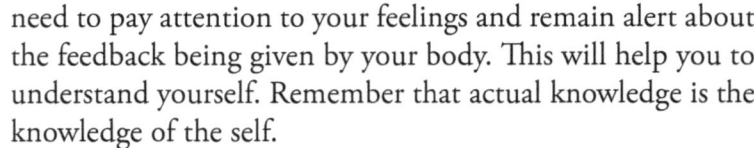

need to pay attention to your feelings and remain alert about the feedback being given by your body. This will help you to understand yourself. Remember that actual knowledge is the knowledge of the self.

Recognize action signals

Nature is constantly giving us action signals to do something or not to do something. It does not give up after sending guidance just once. It keeps warning us time and again. This is something like the speed breakers we see on the roads near a school. About a hundred meters from the school, the billboard reads: 'School ahead. Drive slowly.' Again after fifty meters, there is yet another billboard: 'Speed breaker ahead. Drive slowly.' In addition, the speed breakers are painted with white stripes to alert people from a distance who did not read the board and did not slow down their vehicle. Furthermore, when someone neither reads the boards nor sees the white stripes, they can become aware by seeing the slowing down of vehicles ahead. Thus, you are being alerted many times in many ways. If you are alert, you will slow down after the first warning itself. But if you are not alert, you will ignore all warnings and bump over the speed breaker in full speed, risking an accident.

While guiding you, nature first gives you a feeling or intuition, then sends a signal, and then gives a thought. Supposing you are going to do something and your inner voice warns you against it. And if it warns you not just once or twice, but thrice, then you better take heed of it. This is nature's way of telling you, in all seriousness, not to undertake that task.

> A man approaches his scooter. The scooter almost falls down while taking it off its stand. Remember, the man hasn't even started the scooter yet. This is the first signal. Then he starts it and increases its speed to more than average and almost gets hit by a passing vehicle. This is the second message. He continues to drive in the same manner, and after a while, the same thing happens once again. This means that nature is trying to draw his attention to the fact that he needs to slow down his speed.

This was just an example. We need to note the action signals that we receive such as: 'Stop this; reduce your speed; don't speak in this manner as this tone creates misunderstandings; don't use these words as these words induce fights...' Nature can also remind you of incidents where these words had caused a fight. This denotes that we need to pay attention to these signals and act accordingly for a better life.

Teacher : *You are being punished and still you are laughing!*

Student : *That's because you have taught us that we should laugh even in the face of adversity.*

God : **Don't just laugh; correct your mistakes too.**

Chapter 10

Sixth Step: Become A Plain Paper

Learn how to become eligible for God's autograph

It is only when we become a plain sheet of paper that God can give His autograph to us, i.e. He can express Himself through our body-mind. God signs only on plain paper, whereas we human beings hesitate to sign on a plain paper. This is the major difference between God and man. God says, 'I sign only on plain paper as I reside only in silence, in nothingness.' Becoming a plain paper involves giving up our ego and purifying our mind to make it ready for God's signature. Thus, egoless people who surrender to Him and become pure are eligible to receive His autograph.

God's signature is clearly visible and shines in our being when we erase our ego. Ego is the main hindrance in the flow of divine guidance. God wants to sign on all papers; He wants to give guidance to one and all. It is up to us to be receptive for the guidance. When we become clear and pure, we open up for divine guidance. Let us learn a few steps that will help us in becoming clear and pure, just like a plain paper ready for God's autograph.

1. Take approval from God

Many people seek others' approval for most of the things they do. Before taking any decision, they think, 'Will others approve of it? What will people say if I do this? Will they criticize me?' They are concerned about their impression on others. Even for small things such as buying a new apparel, they take others' opinions. Their decisions depend upon others' consent and they can't take any decision on their own. Ideally, you should seek God's permission before doing anything, not people's. You should tell yourself, 'It doesn't matter if no one in this world approves my decision, but God must approve of it.' As soon as you wake up in the morning, tell yourself, 'Today I am going to do these particular tasks. And this is the way I am going to carry out each task. If there is anything which is not for my highest good, God will stop me at the right moment and my inner voice will guide me towards the right path.' If you begin each day with this thought, you will see that you are being guided appropriately at each step and eventually witness a great change in your life.

Signs of God's approval

You can hear God's approval from within, which is the easiest and the best way. But here's the catch. Man has covered the internal microphone with so many straps over the years that the sound coming from it cannot be heard. God is speaking from within, but the mike is totally covered up. That is why there is need for external guidance. Receiving external guidance in the proper way can help remove the straps muffling the internal mike and you can then hear God's approvals clearly.

When you listen to a discourse from a true guru, you receive wisdom from outside. However, it does not mean you are given something new. The entire wisdom is already within you, only the straps covering the internal mike are removed during the discourse. The external guru helps awaken the internal guru (Consciousness). When your internal microphone is functioning well, you will not need guidance from outside. External guidance only helps in clearing the internal blocks to receive the divine guidance that already exists within as the Consciousness, Self or Truth.

2. Stop looking for reasons; go easy

Man is the only creature on Earth who looks for a reason

behind everything. If he does not get a clear reason for something, he makes assumptions about it. He thereby converts the boon of intellect and imagination into a curse. When animals see different shapes, sizes and states of trees in the forest, they do not ask any questions and accept everything as it is. On the contrary, when we see such scenes, our mind raises a number of questions such as, 'Why is this tree somewhat dry? Why is this one so tall? Why is that one crooked?' When the mind indulges in unwarranted questions owing to its habit of fixing everything in logic, then you must give it the answer: 'Because, it is so.' For instance, when the mind asks, 'Why is this tree so tall?', just say, 'Because it is tall.' That's it. This answer will quiet the mind and stop the train of pointless thoughts. If the mind asks, 'Why was I asked to sit behind?', your answer should be, 'Because I was asked to sit behind.' This is the actual answer to all such questions of the mind. This answer is simple but not so easy to use. With practice, you will learn to give this answer to your mind to stop its ceaseless commentary and the subsequent negative feelings. Note that, at the beginning, the mind will look for logical answers but you must stick to this one.

When you wake up one morning to find a power cut, your mind will promptly question, 'Why is there a power cut?' Just answer, 'Because there is a power cut.' Let's say someone made a face on seeing you, your mind will try to find a number of logical answers to the question, 'Why did he make a face at me?' Just say, 'Because he made a face at me', and apply instant brakes to all those tormenting thoughts. You will be surprised to find that this answer has erased off at least half of your stress there and then.

Don't worry if you cannot use this answer in all circumstances. Having said that, you must at least stop looking for reasons in those situations in which your reasoning depresses you. This will be good for you. You can try to find the reasons if it makes you happy. However, it is not wise to do that if it is going to make you sad. Remember, the wise do not act against their own interests.

We constantly make assumptions in answer to questions such as, 'Why is my neighbour like this? Why is my brother like this? Why did he do this to me? Why did my friend ignore me? Why didn't he remember my birthday? I have no value...' Our mind is often occupied with such questions pertaining to our relations. This drains our energy. We never stop to realize that we are causing so much harm to ourselves by brooding over these thoughts. No other creature on this planet thinks in this manner. That is why only human beings need this training to use the answer 'Because it is so' in order to ease their minds.

You will find that as soon as you stop trying to find the causes and apply the great thought 'This is like this because this is like this,' you will start feeling happy. It is a powerful method to effortlessly eliminate the habit of digging for causes. When you give this answer every time, at the end of the day you will notice that unnecessary thoughts have reduced, and even when some do arise, they are cut off at once. Thus, these types of thoughts stop torturing you and your mind grows calmer. This means that your paper is gradually beginning to become blank. When it becomes totally blank, that's when God's signature will shine on it. That is what we are learning in this chapter.

3. Let go of ego; make way for God

A plain paper indicates an egoless body. God can express Himself best through such bodies. He can actually work full-time through them instead of on a part-time basis. This is because the mind has surrendered and so He can operate 24x7 through that body and not just for a short period as in other bodies where the ego reappears after a short time.

The meaning of ego is the one that says, 'I am separate from all other people. I am special. I am great.' This feeling of being separate is the origin of ego. When this separation dissolves, ego cannot survive and the mind becomes quiet. Thereafter, man considers himself to be only a medium and not the doer. He understands that the doer is God alone, who functions through all the bodies.

Let us understand this through an example. Supposing *Ramleela*, a play based upon the Hindu epic *Ramayana*, is being enacted on stage. One of the characters, under the influence of cannabis, gets excited while watching the scene of Sita's abduction. He storms onto the stage, and to the dismay of the audience, starts hitting Ravana,. Finally, when he sobers down, he realizes that he was bashing the man who was merely playing the role of Ravana. Similarly, when ego falls, we realize that no one is responsible for their actions; all are perfectly playing their roles on the stage called Earth for our training and growth. The story is not ours, nor are the dialogues our own, everything is of God. God is the producer and director of this grand drama and we are just the actors.

4. Get rid of negative tendencies

We cannot hear God's message if our mind is filled with anger, envy, hatred or fear. Therefore, it is important to fill our minds with positive feelings and leave no space for any negative trait. A mind devoid of negative tendencies is like a clean slate, where God's signature is clearly visible.

When you are doing something and thoughts of envy are going on in your mind, you will not be able to think what God wants you to think. Instead, if you are working with a peaceful mind, you may suddenly receive new and different thoughts—thoughts which you have never got before. These are God's thoughts, which can be received only on plain paper.

5. Get rid of misunderstanding and learn your lessons

Man is unaware of the fact that God wants a clean slate. He assumes that God likes to see a lot of writing. He also does not understand that ego is the real cause of all problems in his life, and when he drops it off, he will automatically become a clean slate ready to receive God's signature.

Now the question is, how to become a clean slate? This will happen when your ego goes on reducing while facing the various incidents and stresses of life. Just as coal turns into diamond under pressure, you too can emerge triumphant when put through the problems of life, to achieve your ultimate aim. This is the beauty and also the purpose of this school named Earth.

Challenges in life force you to learn your lessons. Once you have trained your mind and learnt all your lessons, you realize that your 'problems' were actually opportunities in disguise that were meant for your progress.

A : *I used to write letters to my sweetheart each and every day. I even proposed to her in a letter.*

B : *So, what happened? Did she marry you?*

A : *No, she married the postman who used to deliver my letters.*

God : Turn around; where is your attention? On the letter, the writer, or the postman?

Chapter 11

Seventh Step: Learn to Wait

The best way to receive divine guidance

You need to build a pyramid at the seventh step. You must have heard about the pyramids and seen some pictures of them, though you may or may not have visited Egypt. However, here we are not talking about building physical pyramids. Let us see what is meant in the given context. In the word 'pyramid', 'pyra' can be taken to mean prayer and 'mid' as meditation. Thus, the word pyramid represents prayer and meditation. You have to use these two elements to build an internal pyramid that will connect you with God.

Let us further understand how a pyramid of prayer and meditation is built. When you pray for two minutes every hour in the day, say at 07:07, then at 08:08, at 09:09, at 10:10, and so forth, a pyramid is created. Such a pyramid is the ultimate system for connecting with God. You can help God to help you through such prayer and meditation.

Prayer and meditation are the ways in which you can converse with God. And God loves conversing with you. Just as you like to be alone with your own self for some time, God too wants to be alone with you for some time every day. This is possible through prayer, and hence He wants all of us to converse with Him through prayers. When you pray, God listens to you and understands you perfectly. You only need to have faith that your prayers will be answered. Remember, prayer is an ideal way to converse with God, and always have faith in your conversation with God. He knows what is best for you and gives you the best in the best possible manner. The lone obstacle in the path of prayer is the habit of negative thinking.

Prayer and meditation connect you with God and help in elevating your level of awareness. When each prayer is offered with love and gratefulness, and everything given by God is received with love and gratefulness, your level of consciousness rises.

If all the people on Earth pray at the same time, their collective prayers can create miracles. The cause of all the problems prevailing in this world, such as terrorism, racial discrimination, corruption, etc. is low level of consciousness. And, problems cannot be resolved at the same level of consciousness from where they originate. Therefore, to solve problems, we need to raise the level of consciousness of the entire planet. This can be achieved when we work upon our own self. We must pray and meditate every day to reach our inner centre. When our consciousness level rises, we will find new solutions. In other words, new thoughts and new methods will be discovered.

The meaning of reaching the centre

In the epic of *Mahabharata*, when Lord Krishna declared the righteous war, Arjuna was filled with deep sorrow on seeing all his elders, teachers, cousins, friends and relatives in the enemy camp. But despite his sad state, he came to the centre of the battlefield and received guidance from Lord Krishna. Arjuna could have sought the solution without moving to the centre of the battlefield. After all, Krishna was his charioteer, and all Arjuna had to do was to simply ask Him for guidance there itself. Perhaps Arjuna knew that divine guidance cannot be received without reaching the centre—the heart or tejasthan.

We receive guidance only when we reach our centre. In times of stress, we move away from our centre and that's the reason

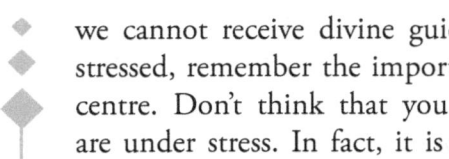

we cannot receive divine guidance. So, whenever you are stressed, remember the importance of coming back to your centre. Don't think that you won't meditate because you are under stress. In fact, it is doubly important for you to meditate during stress. Arjuna was relieved of his stress only after he came to the centre. When you are tensed, do not think that you are in no position to receive guidance. In fact, that is the time when you really need divine guidance; hence move to your centre with prayer and meditation.

Don't cultivate bad habits under stress

During stress, some people feel better after throwing abuses or shouting at others. This is not a good habit. Also, it is not the right way to reduce stress. You should choose a method that can release your stress, and at the same time, save you from falling into bad habits. You must decide in advance what you need to remember during stress. Only then can you find immediate solace and reach your centre.

How can you listen to God's voice when you are away from Him? You cannot. Thus, whenever you are sad or miserable, it means that you are away from God. Likewise, whenever you feel happy, it means that you are close to God.

Whenever you are under stress, you refuse to receive divine guidance. Never ever forget that negative events in life also have a definite purpose. They are actually your growth boosters when you consider them as challenges and face them. They empower you to reach your goals. Conversely, if you do not face the challenges, you become weak and lose your energy. However, it is also crucial to remember that giving undue attention to negative things also saps your energy. Then the question arises: How much attention must be given to them? It is the same as asking, how much salt should be added to a dish? The answer would be, 'Just right; neither less nor more.' You know that if you add too little salt, the food will taste bland, and if you add too much of it, the food will taste like poison. The ingredient that adds taste to a dish can also make it inedible. Therefore, just like the salt in your food, pay just enough attention to a negative event; neither less nor more.

Divine guidance is always available; you just need to signal to God that you are ready for it. You can do that by connecting with your centre. When you pray, you effectively communicate to God or nature — 'I am ready to receive the guidance that is being sent to me. I am receptive for it. Whatever I receive, I will not argue about it. Instead, I will give faith, love and devotion in return; as this will bring the highest good from You to me.' This way you reach your centre with joy.

How to become a magnet

There is a simple technique to become stress free. Recall those moments when you were really happy. How did you feel after your last examination in school or college? How did you feel after successfully completing a big project? Remember your feeling while enjoying a picnic at your favourite spot. Recall the happy moments spent with a loved one. If you can't recall any such moments, just lie down and tell God, 'Please begin Your work. I will not check or interfere.' The human mind is naturally inquisitive and wishes to check everything. It wants to check whether something is happening or not... is my pain reducing or not? Remember, you don't need to check. When you practise this technique during stressful situations, you become a happy magnet again, that attracts all good things in life.

How to pray

Your heart gets closed under stress and you cannot receive divine guidance. You need to be open and happy to receive it. That's why the mission statement 'Whatever you do, do it with a smile' is so important. To increase the intensity of your prayers, you must pray every hour all through your waking hours. If you wake up at 06:00 am, your first hourly prayer would be at 06:06 am. The next one at 07:07, then at 08:08, and so on, until you retire for the night. If you go to bed at 10:30 pm, your last prayer would be at 10:10 pm. You do not have to worry about praying during your sleep hours, because at that time you will naturally be in the experience of the Self. You are always with God in your deep sleep. You lose the awareness of your body during sleep; that is why you don't need to do anything at that time. But you do need to remember to pray during your waking hours. Therefore, make arrangements for timely reminders at every place. Let your watch, cell phone, computer, and everything that can be used, remind you. People around you can also remind you. You enhance your tuning with Mother Nature by praying at a fixed time. Prayers become more effective with tuning. In addition, collective prayers are even more effective than individual prayers.

During your hourly prayer, close your eyes and ask yourself, 'Who am I? How did I do my work in the last one hour? Was I happy, grumbling, or miserable while doing it?' You will receive an answer from within. If the answer is that you had forgotten everything, including your true essence and laughter, don't be unhappy about it. Simply resolve to remember your true essence and to do everything with a smile for the next one hour. This will make you more alert in the next hour. It is possible that you may remember your resolution for the first half an hour and forget it during the latter part of the hour. Don't worry about it. Make the same resolution again during your next prayer. Your awareness level will steadily go on rising.

Pray for world peace

Let us all pray for world peace. We can do it right now. Close your eyes and imagine divine white light falling on the Earth. See all the problems in our world such as recession, terrorism, poverty, hunger, diseases, dowry, murders, violence, religious disputes, pollution, corruption, etc. dissolving in the divine white light. And then see the consciousness of each individual, in fact of the entire planet, rising in the form of golden light emanating from the Earth.

During this prayer, those who could visualize the above description are Ms. Eyes. Those who liked the words in this prayer are Mr. Ears. And those who felt the energy of the light are Dr. Feelings. You can check for yourself as to what you are. Adopt whichever way works for you. Each of them will yield good results.

Synchronization with nature

In the present circumstances of the society at large, it is very important to increase synchronization with nature. Otherwise, it won't be possible to solve the problems of the society. We need to raise the level of our consciousness with every passing hour. We need to maintain our awareness all the time. When all the readers of this message start doing this, the level of consciousness of this planet will rise exponentially. This new level of consciousness will solve all your problems as well as those of the entire planet. Tune yourself to the hourly prayer of remembrance and benefit from it.

You know what happens when there is no synchronization. You may have seen it in some Hindi movies where two brothers who had got separated during childhood now cross one another without looking at each other. In other scenes of the movie, the mother and sons too cross one another, again without noticing each other. All of them meet only at the end of the movie. They could not meet earlier because they were not in sync with each other. The same applies to divine guidance as well. You cannot receive guidance because you are not in sync with nature.

Learn to tune in with nature, else the message may be delivered from one direction and you may be facing the opposite direction. Avoid such a scenario. Align yourself in the right direction. Receive the message as soon as possible, decode it immediately, and start working accordingly. This habit will help you attain whatever you want—be it happiness, love, courage, good qualities, health or wealth.

Until now, you were not given a fixed time for prayer. This is the first time that you have been given a specific time to pray. You have also been told how to pray. This will greatly augment the power of your prayers.

Get into the habit of meditation

Make meditation a daily habit. This will silence the chatter of your mind and clear the path for divine guidance. Meditation will enable you to hear the soft inner voice. Begin with meditation for ten minutes and then maintain the peace you attained during meditation for ten more minutes after opening your eyes. As you start maintaining the peace of meditation even while doing your routine activities, you will gradually find meditation permeating your entire life. This will make you serene and blissful.

Our five senses draw our attention towards external things and invite a variety of ego-based thoughts. This creates a hurdle in receiving nature's messages or divine guidance. When these senses take a backseat and function at a slow pace or become still, the consciousness easily returns unto itself. The Knower becomes the Known and the Witness become the Self-Witness. This is possible only through meditation. Let us learn a powerful meditation technique to experience this. It will also help you receive divine guidance with ease.

Waiting Meditation — preparation for receiving guidance

In today's fast-paced world, the Waiting Meditation teaches you the art of halting for a moment or two. This seems difficult to most people, who think, 'The race is going on just fine, so why should I stop even for two minutes? I may unnecessarily lose speed and it will then take time to catch up again.' When man sees something, he cannot stop himself. He gets lost in it. Sometimes, when he cannot control his anger, he creates a lot of trouble. For this reason, the habit of halting for some time is good for his well-being, which he can learn with the help of Waiting Meditation.

Stopping yourself for two minutes, while on the run, is a great art. Don't undermine this art. It can save you from many sufferings. After learning this Waiting Meditation, you will say, 'These two minutes were highly effective in my life. I could take right decisions because of these two minutes. All the positive things got attracted to me because of these two minutes. Thank God for this wisdom.' Let us now learn this meditation technique.

1) Choose a comfortable place and posture. Close your eyes.

2) Slowly repeat to yourself, 'I am ready to receive divine guidance. I am receptive.'

This meditation is known as Waiting Meditation because you wait for the next thought to appear. You ask the question as to from where would the next thought appear. You then simply wait and watch for the source of the next thought.

3) Keep your body straight but not stiff. Just wait for the next thought. Would it originate from sound?

4) Listen to all the sounds around you. Be aware from where a thought appears. Sitting and waiting in this manner puts a stop to the train of thoughts. Even if a thought does arise, just acknowledge it and ask yourself, 'Where will the next thought come from?' Soon you will learn that thoughts do not arise from external sounds.

5) Next, pay attention to your breath coming in and going out. Check if thoughts come with your breath.

6) The answer will be, 'No, the thought does not arise from our breath.' Continue to track the origin of thoughts.

7) If there is any pain in the body, see if the thoughts are arising from there. Examine your entire body. Pause at the painful spots and ask if the next thought is originating from there.

8) After observing your body pains, move your attention to the sensations on the body. Check the pressure points, warm areas, itchy areas; and see if the thoughts are originating from there.

9) Whenever a thought arises, acknowledge it and move on to see where the next thought is coming from. Is it appearing from the fragrance that your nose can smell? Is it coming from the taste on your

tongue? Wait and see where the next thought is coming from. Where is the source of all thoughts?

10) After a while, open your eyes and look at the objects in the room in which you are seated at present. As you look at each object, ask yourself, 'Is the thought coming from this thing?' Look at another object and ask, 'Will the next thought emerge from this object? Is this object the source?'

11) If you get bored with this process, ask yourself, 'What is the source of this boredom? Where did this thought of boredom come from? Where will the next thought come from?' Wait and watch.

12) Now get up and walk around. Look at each object and ask, 'Will this object give me the next thought?' Remain neutral and look at everything around you. Look at the objects but do not get into their history. Do not worry whether a thought arises or not. Just wait without any conditions or expectations to know where the next thought originates from.

13) Look at the floor, walls and the ceiling. Look to the right and then to the left. Look in front and at the back. Look up and down. If none of these things are giving you thoughts, sit down and close your eyes again. Look at the blank space within, which feels like nothing. Check if the thought is originating from there.

14) 'This *nothing* is not nothing'—you will develop this conviction while you wait. It is only through your body that you know that you are beyond the body.

15) 'Where will the next thought come from?' With this thought pay attention to the source of thought. The Truth will be revealed in this waiting period. Just wait unconditionally and enjoy the process. A lot is happening in this waiting period. Slowly open your eyes with the conviction that a lot is transpiring in the invisible realm.

This meditation helps in stopping the incessant stream of superfluous thoughts. You develop the understanding: 'I, the real me, am the source of all thoughts, and not my senses. I get these particular thoughts because of my beliefs and assumptions.' After this understanding, the mind becomes receptive to nature's messages. Your attention gets diverted from people, objects and environment, and you start decoding God's messages.

Two deaf friends happened to meet on the way and started conversing.

First friend : Hello! What's up? Are you going to the temple?

Second friend : No, I am going to the temple.

First friend : Oh, that's fine, I thought you were going to the temple.

God : **Don't make assumptions; listen completely. Turn your mind within.**

Chapter 12

How To Receive Divine Guidance

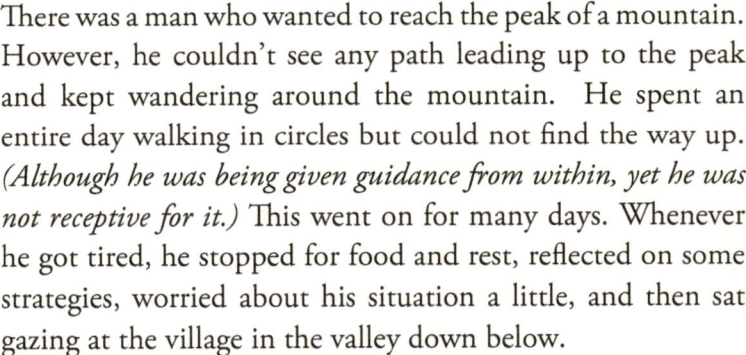

There was a man who wanted to reach the peak of a mountain. However, he couldn't see any path leading up to the peak and kept wandering around the mountain. He spent an entire day walking in circles but could not find the way up. *(Although he was being given guidance from within, yet he was not receptive for it.)* This went on for many days. Whenever he got tired, he stopped for food and rest, reflected on some strategies, worried about his situation a little, and then sat gazing at the village in the valley down below.

From his vantage point, he could see many scenes in that village, such as some people were busy cultivating their land, some were shouting political slogans and indulging in violence, some others were playing music and singing, while some children were flying kites. He watched all this and then wondered, 'What is it that I need to do?' He was not sure of the direction he should take. So, he kept circling the mountain. Whenever he looked at the village, he lost his focus as he listened to the songs being played or saw the political flags fluttering in the wind.

At last, he got sick of roaming around in this manner and prayed, 'Dear God, what should I do to reach the peak? Do I have to keep going around in circles?' (*Most of us go around in circles as well — from office to home, home to office, from home to the market, from home to school or college, and again back home!*) Such thoughts occupied his mind all the time and these thoughts too became his prayer. As a result, he started receiving the internal guidance, which had been coming from the very beginning. It said, 'Sit down and face the mountain that you are circling. Stop looking at the village. Look at the mountain. Meditate while looking at it.'

The man paid heed to this intuition and sat down in meditation looking at the mountain. Lo and behold! This attention started creating a tunnel through the mountain! This development amazed him and encouraged him. He went on increasing the duration of his meditation. The first day he had given it just five minutes, the next day he increased it to ten minutes, and then to fifteen minutes, and so forth. Gradually, he observed that as his meditation time was increasing, the tunnel was simultaneously developing further inside and he was receiving further guidance. (*When an individual's attention is turned inwards, he begins to see such startling things inside and outside which although present all along were not visible to him.*)

The man also realized, 'Someone is there on the other side of the mountain. Whatever I do, he does the same.' He didn't know that this other person was God Himself. When he was circling the mountain, God was doing the same. When he was looking at the village, God too was looking at the village. That's why he hadn't met God yet.

Both had walked the same path for years, yet he had been unable to meet God. But the day he attuned himself with his inner voice and started paying attention to the mountain, his proximity to God increased.

It is the law of nature: *What you pay attention to, multiplies and comes to you.* The same thing happened with this man. As

he sat in meditation, God too sat in meditation on the other side. When his meditation and attention to the mountain created a tunnel of one inch, God's attention created a tunnel of ten inches on the opposite side!

When an individual works, he calculates and anxiously thinks, 'Only one inch can be dug in one day. This is such a huge mountain, it will take many years!' The day he comes to know that he is being assisted from the other side, he becomes carefree. He knows that when he takes one step, God takes ten steps. This creates confidence and faith in him. He starts meditating sincerely and regularly. On the other hand, if he doesn't develop this faith, he often neglects his meditation. He thinks that only one inch of the tunnel is going to be dug, which is not going to help. He cannot see the work that is happening behind the scenes, in the invisible realm.

We don't like to work on things we cannot see. We keep working at things that we can see and try to go on expanding them. This is our weakness. Don't let this weakness deter you from your goal. Convert this weakness into your strength. Tell yourself, 'Even though I can't see it, a lot is happening in the invisible realm during my meditation.'

Suppose you sit in meditation for ten minutes. After ten minutes your mind will say, 'I sat for ten minutes, but nothing happened!' At such times, you must remind your mind that a great deal has happened from God's side which it cannot see. Gradually, a time will come when only a distance of one inch will be left as the tunnel is being dug from both sides. Even at this time, man has no inkling that now only a short distance is remaining and the tunnel is going to be completed very soon. He is not aware that this momentous feat is going to be accomplished in the very next moment. Even a wall of one inch seems like a herculean task because he cannot see that hardly any distance is left between both sides. Consequently, he loses his patience and takes such decisions which he is going to regret later on. Through this story, you are being asked not to make such mistakes in your life. Have faith in the invisible and carry on your work with persistence and perseverance.

The one inch tunnel that you dig every day is enough signal for God to dig ten inches. This is how you are helping God to help you. When you sit in meditation every day, you dig one inch of the tunnel every day—this tunnel will take you from the head to the heart, i.e. to your centre. At first you will say, 'I don't think anything is happening due to my meditation,' but actually a lot is happening. Just ensure that you practise meditation every day. The day you cover the final distance between you and God, you will encounter God—you will attain God Realization or Self Realization.

The story doesn't end here. The story actually begins when God and the devotee meet because now they can together dig the tunnel upwards! This is possible only with co-creation. And this is how at last man comes to know the way to reach the summit. When you join your hands in prayer, you receive the message that the digging has started upwards. Pyramid yoga, i.e. the combination of prayer and meditation, helps you to journey upwards. Just as man needs God, God too needs man. It is a mutual need which completes the cycle.

Place yourself in this story. Recall your category once again. Are you Mr. Ears, Miss Eyes or Dr. Feelings? If you are Mr. Ears, you can get entangled in the music and songs of the village. If you are Miss Eyes, you can get stuck in the scenes of the village. If you are Dr. Feelings, you can feel unhappy due to the violence and suffering in the village. But the moment you receive divine guidance, the village songs become the song of God or *Gita*. Your attention moves from regular scenes to the beauty of nothingness within. Instead of suffering, you start feeling love and compassion.

- Don't focus on violence, shift to benevolence. Don't look down, look up. Crows look down for scraps of food but swans always look upwards. Become a swan. Whatever you do, do it with a smile. Guidance is being given to you through songs, images and feelings. Just be aware.

A man was passing through a graveyard. He looked at a tombstone that

read : Here lies a lawyer, an honest man.

He was surprised and thought, 'Is there such a shortage of space that they have buried two men together in one grave?'

God : Are the political leaders, lawyers, doctors and teachers of today losing the trait of honesty? If so, please revive it.

Chapter 13

Recognize The Sign Language

Signs are always positive

One of the ways nature provides guidance is through signs. Man lives in the world of his thoughts. Sometimes he is in a state of dilemma, while at other times he is in a negative frame. Sometimes he is envious and jealous, and at other times he is joyous. God stays with him through all his various moods and guides him, 'This is what you must do in this situation… this action can bring in this result…' God or nature is forever guiding us. Many a time nature alerts us through various signs and shows us the right path. Our job is to recognize these signs.

In nature everything is simple; we only have to understand it. The signs too are easy to catch; we only have to be ready to catch them.

How does nature guide us? How can we fathom this guidance? Let us understand this through an example.

> A man has gone for a picnic. While having some snacks, he starts wondering if he had locked his house. This thought starts bothering him. 'Is my house open? What if something happens? What if there is a theft ?' He is stuck as he cannot even go home right away to check the door. So he asks for a sign from nature. He prays, 'Please take care of my house and let me know that you are at it.'

Very soon, some words fell upon his ears: 'I had locked the door…' This is what one lady walking by was telling her companion. Those two were talking about their own stuff, but since this man hears this line when he is eagerly waiting for a sign, he takes it as a sign. He feels that nature is indicating in very clear terms that his house is locked and he need not worry about it. Now he becomes tension free and enjoys his picnic.

This man could decipher the sign because he was waiting for the sign and was alert. When you ask for a sign, you have to remain alert, because the sign can appear from anywhere.

Ask for courage to work according to the signs

When you stop listening to and looking at nature, eventually nature too stops sending signs to you. Gradually, you start feeling as if nothing is going well. When you feel this, that's when you once again learn to listen and see. Slowly, the signs start coming in once again. While working with nature, don't be in a hurry. Don't expect everything to happen at once. Be patient.

Sometimes you receive very clear signs, while at other times the signs are vague. If you want clear signs, just ask, 'I need clearer signs. Give me the eye to see the signs and to recognize them. And give me courage to work according to them.' Signs, courage, and faith together will help you to work in accordance with the divine guidance.

Ask for signs and recognize them. If you don't ask, you won't receive. According to the law of nature, an answer comes only when you ask for it. The answer starts coming the moment we ask for it, but we are unable to grasp it. That's why we keep asking repeatedly. We must be patient and look for the answers.

Answers can appear as signs in any form and that is why it is crucial to recognize them. Don't look for them in just one way. On identifying a sign, pray for courage and faith to work on it. You got to have faith; otherwise you won't trust the message. Lack of faith can pose an obstacle in your path.

Simply trust and say, 'I have prayed. I have asked for a sign. I will receive a sign.'

Nature's sign with numbers

If you start noticing a series of numbers every now and then, take it as a sign. You are walking on the street and a car's number plate catches your eye: 3333. You walk ahead and see another number plate with 2222. Now that's a sign. Perhaps these numbers are telling you to bring synchronization in your prayers, i.e. do not pray for opposite things and also ensure that your thoughts are not contradictory to your prayers, since that will cancel your prayers. The number signs could also convey that the fulfilment of your prayers has begun.

Supposing a particular number keeps popping up from everywhere—in the newspaper, on the television, on the billboard—then it is also a sign. Serial numbers such as 12345 can also be a sign.

Different people, different signs

Different people receive different signs. Sometimes some people receive special signs. This need not happen with everyone though. You must try to observe how you receive the signs. Once you have understood what kind of signs you receive, you can reap its benefit all through your life.

Supposing a man sees the number 425. It happens to be his birth date: 25th of April. This may be a sign for him. Whatever comes to your notice, just wait for a second and ask what sign it is giving. Different things can act as signs for different people. Nature sends messages not only in the form of numbers, but also in other forms. Some may receive a message through a book or a pamphlet. Sometimes you may be praying for someone and then you may hear that very person's name in a conversation of some passerby speaking on the phone. That too is a sign. An image in the clouds can also be a sign. A song can also bring a message.

Decode the message

If you see something unusual, it may be a sign. For example, if you are walking on the road and suddenly you happen to see a butterfly. Remember that this is nature's message. You may see a rare or unusual bird; this could be a sign. You may see a rainbow which is not an everyday occurrence; take it as a sign from nature.

Supposing a man is relaxing at home. He just goes out for a minute to the corner store to buy something, and an unusual scene appears in front of him and then disappears soon after. This scene is nature's message for him. He must recognize and decode the message.

You may hear a meaningful song and get a message. You pray for something and then hear a song on the radio whose words convey that your prayer is being worked upon and you need not worry. For instance, one of your relatives is not well and you are praying for him, 'O Lord! Please bless him and make him well soon. Please give me a sign that my prayer is going to be fulfilled.' At that time, you hear a song which tells you that your relative is on the way to recovery. At other times, you may have noticed that you get to hear the same song again and again, (perhaps other than the one which is a current rage), from every possible source. Please understand that anything that comes into your experience time and again always carries nature's message in it.

Nature is guiding every creature in the world. Everyone is receiving guidance from within as well as from without. All one needs is the art of decoding the messages.

Negative thoughts are not messages

We all need to take various decisions in our life. We often face a dilemma : 'Should I take this or that?'

A student prays, 'O God, should I take up this line of education or that one?' A young man is worried thinking, 'Should I marry this girl or that one?' Another one wonders, 'Should I take up a job or a business?' Yet another person is confused thinking, 'Should I make this deal or not?'

Different people face different dilemmas. At times like these, one should ask for a sign from nature saying, 'Please send me a sign according to my Divine Plan.'

Don't be rigid that a message should arrive in a certain manner only. Also know that nature does not use negative means to send signs to you. Signs are always delivered in positive ways. Negative thoughts are not signs because they are against nature. Don't have any doubt regarding this. Do not look at a negative event and take it as a message. Rest assured that nothing negative is ever related with divine signs.

Receive guidance by becoming a stress free magnet

In order to receive messages easily, you will have to become a 'stress free magnet'. Someone may have asked for a sign from nature, but if he doesn't get a sign for some time, he starts getting anxious. He starts pacing the floor in tension thinking, 'No sign has appeared... it still hasn't appeared...'

This worry becomes an obstacle. If you worry, you can't see even simple signs that are present right before you. The law of signs says: *The calmer you are, the faster you can catch the signs.* Only stress free magnets attract positive things.

Parents almost always worry about their children. If a child is late from school, his parents start panicking. If you are such a parent, ask for signs from Mother Nature instead of worrying. Pray for your child's safety and ask, 'Please give me a sign that my child is safe.' As soon as you receive the sign of your child's safety, you can relax. Then there is no need to worry until your child reaches home.

If you feel that you are not getting the sign, tell yourself, 'Be tension free. Let the worries go... relax... relax...' The excessive desire to receive a sign becomes the obstacle in receiving it. As soon as you become stress free, you will start receiving signs easily. Become a master in catching signs. Whenever you are in a dilemma, pray for signs and courage.

Let us understand the entire process in brief:

Step 1: Ask

Ask for guidance from God or nature, according to your needs, i.e. pray for it. The one who has more problems should pray more often.

Step 2: Remain alert

After asking, remain alert to receive the answer. This is very important. Don't pray and go to sleep (figuratively). Don't live an unconscious life. After praying, stay aware wherever you are, and try to catch the signs. The answer will come to you in one form or the other.

Step 3: Take action

Whatever answers you receive after praying and staying alert, start working on them. Don't just sit idle. For example, if you have prayed for health and someone gives you a book on improving your health, start reading it right away. Don't say, 'I can't read this.' Remind yourself that this is a message specifically sent to you by nature.

Step 4: Review

After receiving the message and taking action on it, review the whole process. In other words, contemplate upon: What was the message? How did I decode it? Was I right? What was the result? In this way, always review your actions.

After reviewing, more answers will come up. Then go back to the first step using these new answers as a base. Offer a new prayer with the new information. New information leads to a new prayer which again leads to a new message followed by a new action and fresh review. This process will make you an expert in decoding signs and receiving guidance from God.

God: Whatever you do, do it with a smile.

Section II
Whatever you do, do it with a smile

If God be with us, who can oppose us?

—Bible

'You don't stop laughing because you are old.

You grow old because you stop laughing.'

—Michael Prichard

'God often visits us;

but more often than not, we are not at home.'*

—*A proverb in French*
*our inner centre/heart

Chapter 14

When Does God Laugh?

Obstacle in the way of laughter

When does God laugh? Does He laugh when someone going to a flour mill to grind wheat says, 'I am going for grinding the flour'? Flour doesn't need any grinding. It is already in powder form. But that is what most people say.

Does He laugh when two people fight and one claims, 'This is my land; a mosque cannot be built here'?

Does God laugh when someone says, 'This is my temple; this temple's land belongs to me, this temple's God is only mine'?

Does God laugh when a lover tells his beloved, 'I will pluck the stars for you'?

Does God laugh when he hears someone say, 'This is my home'? God knows that everyone is just a guest in this world.

Does God laugh when someone spreads the rumour that the world is going to end on a particular date? God knows that the world has just about started opening and blossoming; it has a long way to go. He knows that such people are simply fooling others for their own selfish gains.

Does God laugh when someone says, 'You haven't taken the *prasad*, and hence God will be angry with you'?

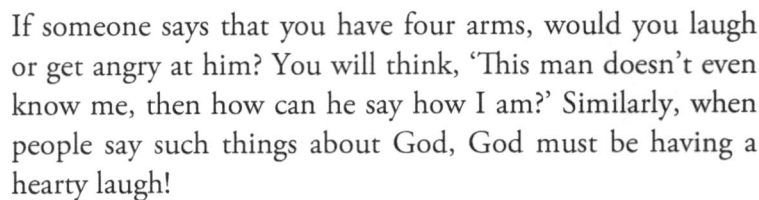

If someone says that you have four arms, would you laugh or get angry at him? You will think, 'This man doesn't even know me, then how can he say how I am?' Similarly, when people say such things about God, God must be having a hearty laugh!

When people draw various portraits of God, does He laugh? When someone says, 'There is delay in God's court but not injustice', what then does God say? Does He say, 'You have never come to my court, then how can you know anything about my court? How do you know what is there or not there? If you want to talk about my court, please visit it sometime. Even when you visit a temple, you don't come inside. There too you behave just like a customer.' You may have seen in some small shops that a customer does not enter the shop; he stands at the counter outside and tells the shopkeeper what he wants. Likewise, man goes to the temple and says, 'Dear God, I need this thing. I need that job. I want a good house and a car. I want my mom to get well...' That's why God says, 'At least come inside my court or my home sometime.'

Have you ever gone to a temple and said, 'Dear God, I don't want anything. I have come here simply to ask about Your well-being. So, how are You? How is Your world doing? Is everything alright?' We never go to a temple just to meet God. Even when we go there, we complain to Him, 'You don't listen to us. You don't answer my questions.'

The truth is that God always answers us, but He does it in His own way. Have we ever devoted time to learn His language? If we want to learn a foreign language, we take up at least a three-month course for that, but we have no time to learn God's language. We always think, 'I will go to God and ask for this thing and come back.' If we had devoted some time to learn His language, we would have asked for God Himself from God, instead of asking for material objects. That would have given us real happiness and our laughter would have been real too.

Beliefs — the obstacle in the way of laughter

How do you imagine God to be? What kind of illusion do you live in because of this imagination?

We have so many beliefs in our mind regarding God. Some examples are: If I do this work on a Monday, this particular God will get angry, if I do it on a Tuesday, this other God will get angry. If I eat anything sour on a Friday, this Goddess will get angry. If I get my hair trimmed on a Saturday, Lord Shani will get angry.

There are innumerable beliefs prevalent in all parts of the world. People lead their lives with these beliefs, without questioning, 'Why would God get angry? God is love. Can love get angry with anyone? Can water's wetness ever end?' Just as water cannot be 'not wet' because wetness is its intrinsic attribute, in the same way God too cannot be angry or 'not love' as love is His intrinsic attribute.

Man has created his own imaginary tales about God and His anger. The truth is that God has never got angry with anyone till date. If He were ever to get angry, He will be angry about the fact that man thinks God gets angry. Since man gets angry, he believes that God too must be getting angry just like him. There is absolutely no shred of truth in this belief.

Man carries many such beliefs and propagates them, such as: 'If a cat crosses your path, it's a bad omen. If your palm itches, you will receive money. If your eye twitches, something bad will happen. This day is auspicious; that particular day is inauspicious...' Thanks to these beliefs, man is bereft of real joy and laughter.

Do you want to have true laughter? The reality is that eternal, unbroken bliss is your innate nature. You are a swan and you can laugh. God is the consciousness that gives you the feeling of being alive. God is beyond form, colour, or shape. Just as a transistor radio cannot function without a battery, we cannot function or even exist without God. God is our life. We need to integrate this truth. Truth and God are inside us. The joy that you attain on imbibing this truth will keep growing with time. It won't reduce. If you have faith in God, you will start receiving the evidence of this.

Boy	:	*If one sits on the moon and prays, God can hear the prayers real fast.*
Girl	:	*Why's that?*
Boy	:	*From the moon, it's a local call.*
God	:	**Please don't make any presumptions about God.**

Chapter 15

God Laughs Or Cries: Depending Upon Your Faith In Him

When to laugh out loud

Have you developed the conviction that laughter is your nature or do you believe in spending your life with a long face? There is another law of nature that states: *Whatever you believe in, you receive its proof.*

If you believe that people are bad, you will receive its proof by meeting people who treat you badly. If you believe there isn't enough money or that people do not return borrowed money, you will receive its proof by experiencing lack of money and people will actually borrow money from you and not return it.

Are you convinced that people do not behave properly with you? That they don't pay attention to you? Perhaps you are carrying these beliefs since childhood. Perhaps you were always asked to stay back while playing games. Such incidences may have made an impression in your mind that you will always be behind others. Perhaps you are living with this belief even now. Your well-wishers may have tried to persuade you otherwise that you are not less than anyone and are equal to or even greater than others, yet you won't listen. You don't trust anyone but your own beliefs. And as you believe, accordingly your conviction on it goes on getting stronger and so do its manifestations.

An old woman had heard about the power of prayer. She was told that one can get whatever one asks by praying — so much so that even a mountain can move if asked with deep faith. That old woman thought of trying it out, thinking, 'Let me see if God hears my prayer or not!' She prayed that night, 'The mountain on the south of my house should relocate to the east. If this happens by morning, I will believe in the power of prayer; otherwise prayer won't mean a thing to me.' Saying so, she went off to sleep. In the morning, she woke up and rushed out to check. The mountain had not moved an inch. She exclaimed, 'Ha! I knew it!! A mountain cannot move. I already knew there is no such power in prayer.'

If you pray with that kind of conviction, your prayer will never be fulfilled. Perhaps this lady did not know the importance of faith in prayer, otherwise she would not have prayed in that manner.

God, man, and laughter

Why did God associate with man?

1. For laughing
2. For crying
3. For both, laughing and crying

Some people think that God associated with man for laughing, and others think for both, laughing and crying.

Those who think that God connected with man for both laughing and crying are asked the next question:

1. Did God connect with man to laugh more and cry less?
2. Did God connect with man to cry more and laugh less?

Now they may answer that God would prefer to laugh more. Remember that you will receive the evidence of whatever you believe in. This is the power of thoughts. Happy thoughts will bring you the proof of happiness. 'I have everything in abundance.' If that is what you believe, then that is what you shall have. But you should believe it with all your heart. Whatever you believe deeply will actualize—whether positive or negative.

Now another question arises: Whose will must be fulfilled:

1. Man's—individual aspirations?

2. God's—expression of Truth / Consciousness?

If you want God's will to be fulfilled, then whenever you feel like crying during sorrow or during a challenging situation, ask yourself, 'Whose desire must be fulfilled—mine or God's?' If you have faith and devotion for God, you will say, 'God's desire must be fulfilled.' If God's desire is to be fulfilled, you must laugh under all circumstances because that is God's will. Tears appear only due to ignorance. God did not unite with the human body in order to cry. He did so to feel happy and laugh and express Himself by creating various new creations through our body. With this understanding, let us make His wish come true and let Him express freely through us.

If God wants to laugh through us, then why not laugh aloud?

A man on	:	*Did you read the false news of my death in today's the phone newspaper?*
His friend	:	*Yes, but where are you calling from—heaven or hell?*
God	:	**People remain stuck in illusion even after hearing the truth.**

Chapter 16

Man's Inherent Nature: Laughter

Animal and Man

You may have seen some people who are forever whining and complaining. Some people always look grim and serious. Some people don't laugh much, but there are some who can be seen laughing very often.

People look at the last category of individuals and ask with a wrinkled brow, 'Why do you laugh so much?' This question says a lot about the state of our country, our society, and our world at large. A society in which laughter is questioned must definitely be in a pathetic condition.

When someone laughs, he is simply behaving in accordance with his inherent nature. That's why when people ask him why he is laughing, he wonders, 'Why can't I laugh without any reason?' The irony is that no one ever asks, 'Why are you not laughing? Have you forgotten your basic nature?' The 'why' question is asked only when someone laughs.

Today the world is in such a condition that we need a reason to laugh. A reason could be that someone is blessed with a child after a long wait, someone gets promoted at work, or clears an examination, or recovers from a sickness. We all know such reasons. But do we actually need a reason? Can't we laugh without a reason?

When a mother is asked, 'Why do you love your child?' she says, 'It's in my nature to love; and I don't need reasons to love my child!' Likewise, laughter is your innate nature. When you laugh spontaneously, and when you love yourself and others, you are in sync with your nature.

Difference between man and animal

There are two main differences between man and animal:

1. Man can think but animals cannot. Man uses the faculty of thought and that is why he labels things and people as good or bad. But an animal cannot think, so it does not label anything either—it doesn't even know whether it is a donkey or a monkey! Man is different from other animals because of his thinking power. This power also makes him the leader of the pack.

2. The second difference is that man can laugh. Man is a laughing creature. He has the boon of laughter and that is why he is different from other animals.

God has blessed man with the attribute of laughter, which has made him more special. Joy and laughter is the only thing that can make man reach the Truth or the Experience of Being; and that is what every man is actually seeking. When we laugh, we don't oblige anyone, we only express our basic nature, we only express the joy which is inside us. When we remember the Truth (our truth, our true nature), then laughter will manifest in the real sense and we will know that everyone in this world is entitled to laugh.

Who is entitled to laugh?

Does a doctor think that he cannot laugh because he has to be constantly on-call for his patients at any hour of the day or night? His life is not like other people's life. His first duty is to serve mankind. He cannot enjoy sound sleep at night. Does that mean he cannot laugh?

Does a teacher think, 'The students nowadays are undisciplined and rowdy. Sincere study is not anywhere on their list. My entire life has been wasted trying to make them see reason. In such conditions, I simply cannot laugh.'

Do students think that they are not entitled to laugh because they have teachers who are more interested in punishing them rather than teaching them?

Does a father think that he has no right to laugh because his son is a useless fellow, who neither studies nor works?

Does a wife think, 'My husband never takes me on an outing or to a movie, how can I laugh?'

Does a husband think, 'My wife keeps demanding something or the other every day, how can I laugh?'

Does a farmer think, 'It doesn't rain on time, the crops are not good, I grow food but don't have enough to eat, and I don't get a good price for my yield. How can I laugh?'

Does a policeman continually think about criminals, hooligans, rapists, thefts and murders, and conclude that he has no right to laugh?

Does a political leader think that nowadays there are so many riots taking place in the name of religion, and hence he is not entitled to laugh?

Does a lawyer think that there is always deception going on in the name of the law and that's the reason he does not have the right to laugh?

Does a businessman think that there is always a risk of recession in business and that's why he has no right to laugh?

No man can ever say, 'I am a doctor [or lawyer, student, wife, etc.] and that's why I have no right to laugh.' Each man has the full right to laugh, because laughter is man's inherent trait. Just as water's nature is to be wet and to flow, man's true nature is to laugh. No one has ever seen dry water. If you tell water, 'You are always wet, that's so great of you,' the water will reply, 'I am not great, this is my nature.' You too must know your nature. You should know that you don't need a reason to laugh.

Supposing a person is told that those who laugh will not get any prize, only those who don't laugh will get a prize. This person will think, 'I must have got it wrong. The one who laughs should get a prize and not the other way round.' That's when he will be told that laughter itself is the biggest reward. Those who cannot laugh deserve pity, that's why they will be given some prize so that they will feel happy and laugh.

Those who laugh without any conditions do not think, 'I will laugh so that I get a prize, or so that my desires get fulfilled, or so that I get a job, or so that my watch starts ticking…' Instead they say, 'Laughter and joy are our prime gifts.'

Laughter is your natural trait. It is a divine gift. It helps in your all-round growth due to which you will always feel joyous. You will get filled with happy and higher thoughts. This is what will take you to the peak of supreme success and help you achieve the highest goal of your life.

After learning the secret of laughter, you understand that God has endowed man with the wealth of laughter and hence he is fully entitled to laugh anytime and anyplace. No man can ever say that he has some problem, some stress, some illness, and therefore he cannot laugh. When a happy man was asked, 'Why do you laugh?' he said, 'I laugh to stay healthy.' He was further asked, 'Why do you want to stay healthy?' He laughed and said, 'So that I can laugh even more and enjoy my life fully and truly.'

In the next chapter, we shall understand various types of laughter and learn what true laughter is.

Customer : *Have you ever shaved a donkey?*
Barber : *No, please sit down; I'll give it a try.*
God   : Teasing someone is not true laughter.

Chapter 17

First Laughter: Lip Laughter

Criticism and Comments

Laughter originates from deep within a person and appears on his face. That is true laughter. There is false laughter too but it has no roots. It is like a plant which has dried and fallen off for want of nutrition.

A happy man is friendly. He is liked by everyone. A crying man cries alone. He is a burden to all. If you wish to win people's hearts, learn to laugh.

There are three kinds of laughter in man's life. The first kind of laughter is the lip laughter, the second one is the head laughter, and the third one is the heart laughter.

First laughter: Lip laughter

The first type of laughter is the lip laughter. This is a false laughter. In this kind of laughter, people enjoy laughing at others by troubling, hurting, teasing, imitating, gossiping, criticizing, or making fun of others.

When some people laugh, others too join in their laughter. This too is lip laughter. For instance, if someone hears a joke but laughs without understanding it, that is a false laughter. Such people see others laughing and start laughing themselves. But this laughter is limited only to the lips. If someone tickles you, you laugh, but that too is lip laughter.

People, who laugh from the lips alone, laugh by deriding others. They enjoy this laughter. A student tells his teacher, 'There is a madhouse in the city. On the first floor only those patients reside whose every answer is, "I know." On the second floor are those patients who always say, "I don't know." Sir, do you know this story?' The teacher says, 'No, I don't know.' The student quips, 'This means you are from the second floor!' The teacher understands his pupil's game and says, 'Oh, is that so? Do you know what the residents of the third floor do? The residents of the third floor narrate this story to everyone! So, dear boy, we are all in the same madhouse. Don't ever think that you are outside it.'

In this way, some people think of themselves to be distinct and superior to others. They think that they are great, but the truth is that all the people in this world are great. Everyone is a swan, but we get fooled by the external appearances. If we stay stuck in the outer form, we cannot laugh a true laughter. When we look at everyone from the higher angle of the Self, only then will our laughter be true. What kind of laughter was the above-mentioned student looking for? He was trying to prove that everyone belongs to the madhouse, except him. This gave him false happiness, which eventually will result in suffering and misery.

Such people love to pull others' legs. These kind of students are found in every school, college, and classroom. They like to say insulting things and pass comments about others. All other children laugh at their antics and they feel happy. This is the first kind of laughter which is called the lip laughter.

Such people have many other methods to trouble others and laugh, such as they will write a letter to someone: 'I had written a letter to you earlier. Please ignore it as I don't know what all I wrote in it... which I shouldn't have.' The truth is that such a letter was never written, but the person receiving the letter will wonder about that first letter... what all it may contain? He will ask everyone at home and office if there had been a letter for him. He will feel anxious about it.

People also harass others over the phone. A man dials a number and says, 'Please give the phone to Mr. Kumar.' The lady on the other end says, 'Mr. Kumar doesn't live here,' and puts the phone down. The man calls again and repeats, 'Sister, give the phone to Mr. Kumar.' The lady now gets irritated and says, 'This is a wrong number. There is no Kumar here.' The man calls the third time and says, 'Give the phone to Mr. Kumar.' Now the lady loses her patience. She screams, 'I have told you so many times that there is no Kumar here,' and bangs the phone down. Even after this the man is not satisfied. He calls once again and says, 'Hello, I am Kumar. Was there a call for me?'

Such people laugh after troubling others via phone, letters, or poor jokes. This is false laughter, which comes from the lips alone. There is no joy in this laughter. Rather, the person on the receiving end gets troubled by it. When real laughter is lost, this is what remains. Thus, you have understood now that many people are stuck in false lip laughter. We will learn about head laughter in the ensuing chapter.

Wife : *I think it's an earthquake! The walls are shaking.*

Husband : *Honey, there's nothing to worry about. We don't own this house, we live on rent.*

God : **A foolish man's logic increases foolishness. A fool's company can even prove fatal.**

Chapter 18

Second Laughter: Head Laughter

The Secret of Laughter

Head symbolizes the intellect. It has three departments: imagination, memory, and power of discrimination (*viveka*). Some people laugh aloud because the doctor has told them that they will be healthy if they laugh. These people laugh to attain or maintain good health. This is head laughter.

Some people laugh while imagining something. When a joke is told they laugh a lot, while some others do not laugh as much. People who laugh more do so because they can imagine a lot more. They visualize the event which is being narrated in the joke and crack up.

> Two friends were going to the market. One of them saw a fat woman passing by and started laughing. His laughter grew louder and then he simply could not stop laughing. His friend was astonished. 'Why are you laughing so hard? What's the matter?' Holding his sides, he said, 'That fat woman was my classmate in college.' His friend was puzzled. 'So what?' He replied, 'While in college, I had proposed to her but she had declined. Now I am laughing in joy, thanking God for her refusal. Otherwise you can imagine what would have been my condition with her now!'

Thus, this man was exultant creating castles in the air, just like the famous character Sheikh Chilli, who used to sit and imagine, 'These eggs will hatch. I will sell the chickens and buy goats. Then I will sell goats and buy a cow. I will sell cow's milk and earn money. I will build a mansion and keep many servants. They will all be at my beck and call...' Similarly, people make such castles in the air and feel delighted.

There are some people who don't laugh even after hearing a joke. Later they go home and laugh. When the joke was told to them, they couldn't understand it. After reaching home they understand, 'Oh, so this was what the joke meant!' and they laugh. There are others who laugh twice. First when they see others laugh at the joke (they laugh because everyone is laughing). Then they laugh once again at home, when they actually understand the joke. Sometimes they laugh a third time as well, when they recall the joke and feel, 'Oh, it was such a simple joke but I couldn't understand it then.' Thus, there are many people who laugh many times on a single joke.

The third department of the intellect is the power of discrimination or discriminative intelligence. It also means understanding. Some people laugh because they understand the Truth. This laughter is of a higher kind. The lip laughter is not a higher kind.

The secret of laughing all the time

> There was a man who was always cheerful. People asked him, 'What is the secret of your happiness?' He replied, 'When my mother was on her deathbed, she gave me a teaching. It is due to that teaching that I always remain happy.' 'What was this teaching?' 'Well, my mother had said, "Son, if you stop laughing because of change in people, environment, or business, it means you have been defeated by them."' This man did not want to be defeated. Even if his favourite object broke or anything else happened, his laughter continued. In other words, he did not change with external circumstances. He was not defeated by defeat.

Laughter is not something external; it is an inner matter, a matter of the heart. If the laughter inside you is lost, it means you have been defeated. The man in the above example lived his entire life with laughter, thanks to just this one doctrine. If a man has learnt how to laugh, he has learnt how to win.

This kind of laughter is known as laughter of discrimination. Discrimination means understanding the difference between truth and untruth. A man who laughs this laughter knows the difference between real and false laughter. Beyond real and false laughter is *Bright Laughter*, just as *Bright Knowledge* is the ultimate wisdom beyond knowledge and ignorance, *Bright Silence* is the supreme silence beyond sound and silence, and *Bright Happiness* is the unremitting bliss beyond joy and suffering.

Only those people have the right to laugh at others who can laugh at themselves. An intelligent man knows this truth through understanding. The one who laughs at others' mistakes should ask himself, 'Do I laugh at my own mistakes?' Laughing at your own mistakes is a higher level of laughter.

Biggest mistake, loudest laughter

When we laugh at our own mistakes, higher understanding begins and our discriminative intelligence awakens. We then start thinking, 'Who am I?' Man lives his entire life assuming himself to be the body. You say, 'This is my shirt. This is my vest. This is my house.' Whenever you say the word 'my' it means that you are not that thing. 'My house' means that I am not the house. In the same context, when you say 'my body,' it means that I am not the body. But despite that, you still consider yourself to be the body!

This is the biggest mistake. How much should you laugh at this blunder! But no one laughs at it. Unless you laugh at this mistake, you will not receive higher understanding. Discriminative intelligence says, 'Laugh at your mistake on seeing how soon you forget that you are not the body.'

The moment you wake up in the morning, you remember all that you have to do throughout the day: 'I have to make tea and breakfast, I have to do the laundry, I have to go to the office...' But you don't remember that the one who goes to the office is your body. You always think, 'I have to go to the office.' You start committing this mistake in the morning itself. If someone reminds you that the one going to the office is your body, not you, how much would you laugh?

To live like a swan means knowing the Truth and awakening the power of discrimination. This will give birth to such laughter that all suffering will seem like an illusion.

Some people laugh to pester others. Such laughter is in vain. Only that laughter is worth something which makes others happy and arouses laughter in them. When will every person become happy? Let us understand this through a story.

> There was a joker in a king's court. He used to do all kinds of crazy stuff and speak rubbish. He would say whatever he felt like and all the courtiers would laugh at his jokes. Some people like that laughter which is triggered by words. When the words are jumbled up, it amuses them. If someone stutters or uses wrong words, they burst into laughter.

Supposing some unexpected guests suddenly arrive at a lady's house. She wants to tell her son, 'There is a cat in the room. Get it out and make the guests comfortable.' But in a hurry she says, 'Get the guests out of the room and make the cat comfortable.' All those who hear these words break into splits. Such people find jumbled words to be totally hilarious. But true joy lies beyond words.

> So, the court jester used to provide the courtiers with the fun of words. He used to tell jokes which made everyone double up with laughter.

> One day, he made some mistake while telling a joke. This angered the king. In his anger he declared, 'Tomorrow you will be hanged!' As happens in every place, in the royal court too, many courtiers were jealous of the jester. The king's declaration gladdened their hearts.

Later, when the king had calmed down, he realized that he had ordered death for his favourite clown. This was a big mistake. He wanted to make amends. The next day he went into the court and told the clown, 'You have served me well for many years; hence I give you the freedom to choose the mode of your death. Tell me, how would you like to die—by hanging, drowning, or being pushed down from a mountain?' The jester fell into deep thought. He didn't want to die. Using his intelligence and discriminative power, he said, 'I want to die of old age.' This answer pleased the king very much because he too did not want him to die. No one in the court could help but laugh at this clever but critical answer.

Thus, at the end of the story, we understood how the court jester by using his intellect and discrimination at the right time saved his life and generated higher laughter in the court. The laughter originating from the intellect and discrimination delights everyone. This laughter is higher laughter. How can we bring such laughter into our lives? This can be understood by understanding heart laughter.

Priest : *Alcohol is our enemy. Don't ever touch it.*

Drunkard : *Why? You have told us that we should love our enemy!*

God : **Don't misuse your intellect. Don't imbibe substances that corrupt your intellect.**

Chapter 19

Third Laughter: Heart Laughter

Stomach or eyes

The third kind of laughter is the heart laughter, which is also known as *Bright Laughter*. It originates from the *tejasthan*, the centre, the heart.

Do you take a plunge into your heart before laughing? Do you take a dip in the silence within?

If you do, your laughter is heart laughter, because silence and laughter are two sides of the same Truth. You regard the outer silence to be real silence. If someone is quiet, you say he is in silence. However, that silence is not real silence. He may be externally quiet but there can be a storm of thoughts raging in his mind. That is why it cannot be termed as silence. When laughter takes a dip into the ocean of silence within and emerges, it is called heart laughter.

Say, someone dips his finger in honey and licks it, what a sweet taste he will get! Now if someone licks his finger without dipping it in honey, he obviously won't get any taste. The laughter which does not originate in silence is empty laughter. We need to learn: How does laughter spring from the heart? What is in the heart? What does one have to learn from the heart? How can one reach the heart (tejasthan or centre)? How can you receive the light?

The eyes are the mirror of your heart

We can recognize laughter through the eyes because eyes do not lie. They indicate the type of our laughter. Eyes are the mirror that reveal the truth of our heart. Outwardly, we may say, 'I am very happy,' but our eyes convey what kind of joy we have—whether our joy has originated from the lips, from the intellect, imagination, memory, discrimination or heart! You can recognize heart laughter through the eyes because eyes are the checking point.

The other way to identify laughter is through the belly. When some people laugh, their belly starts shaking but everyone's belly is not that big to let others see their laughter. Therefore, eyes remain the real indicators of laughter.

Thus, we have understood that heart laughter is the highest laughter.

Mr. Mind   :   *Is laughter very expensive in the market?*
Mr. Smiles :   *No, actually there is a shortage of laughter.*
God   :   **Search for your true laughter.**

Chapter 20

Laughter Experiment

Listen to your laughter

You can experience your laughter with the help of an experiment. Let us understand this with an anecdote.

> Once, a man had gone to listen to a lecture which was to be delivered by the manager of his company. When he returned home, his wife asked him, 'How was the lecture today? Hope you didn't get too bored.' The man replied, 'The manager failed to turn up; so they made *me* speak on the stage.' Surprised, his wife said, 'Oh, really? So, you gave the lecture. Did people enjoy your lecture or did they get bored?' The man said, 'I don't know... I didn't hear my lecture. I became nervous on the stage, so I couldn't hear anything that I said.'

Have you ever heard your own lecture, or your own laughter? Whenever you laugh, you cannot hear your laughter because your attention is always directed outwards. There is a law of nature that states: 'Whatever you give attention to, grows in your life.' When parents give attention to their children, they grow, blossom, and become healthy. On the other hand, if children are neglected, their health and character is ruined.

Having understood that, try this laughter experiment at home. In this experiment, laugh for 15 seconds. See yourself laughing and listen attentively to your laughter. When you experience your laughter, your laughter will increase. You will open up and blossom, and be able to laugh openly. During this experiment, whenever you laugh, listen to your own laughter, not that of others'.

We may have laughed so many times till date, but we may have hardly heard our laughter. Stop reading this book for a minute and laugh out loud (if you are alone). Listen to your laughter. Pay attention to it. Today science has proved that people who laugh can easily tolerate suffering and also recover faster from any disease. Laughter is an established remedy and a general tonic for your physical, mental, emotional, and spiritual health. That is why many laughter clubs have sprung up in many cities where people can get together, laugh out loud, and also listen to their laughter.

So, wherever possible, listen to your own laughter. Remember the law: 'Whatever we pay attention to grows in our life.' The more attention you give to your laughter, the more it grows. As you believe, so are the proofs you receive. If you believe that life is for changing, growing and laughing, that's what you shall see. If you believe that life is an ocean of suffering, that's what you shall see.

With this laughter experiment, you will experience a new consciousness within you.

Disciple : *Why do you laugh without any reason?*

Zen master : *Laughter drives monkeys away.*

Disciple : *But there are no monkeys here.*

Zen master : *See, I told you!*

God : **No reason is required for laughter. Only your presence is required.**

Chapter 21

Learn To Laugh At Your Fears and Your Anger

Law of Nature

We have to learn to laugh at our fears, worries, anger, and follies. This is because laughter acts like a balm for each of these illnesses. Very few people know how to laugh at their fears. They know that laughter brings all our mental flaws under control.

Supposing someone is afraid of cockroaches. He should try laughing at himself by thinking, 'I am scared of such a tiny creature… hahaha… Can this creature grab me?… hahaha… In fact, it must be scared of me.'

You can lighten a tension-filled environment by laughing at your fears and worries. It is easy to laugh when everything is going hunky dory. Even a fool can laugh under favourable circumstances. That's no big deal. But you need courage to laugh under adverse conditions.

If all your 32 teeth are shining white and you are laughing with your mouth wide open, it's no big deal. But if two of your front teeth are missing, and you can still laugh openly, now that takes courage.

Until now we only knew how to laugh at others. That is as easy as it is difficult to laugh at our own self. Only those people have the right to laugh at others' fears, worries, and troubles, who can laugh at their own. Only those who can laugh at their own mistakes have the right to laugh at others' mistakes.

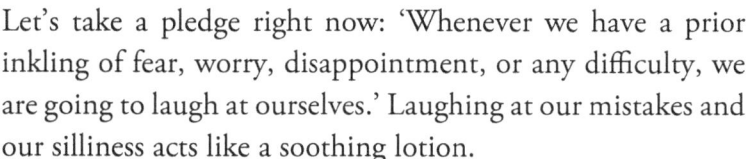

Let's take a pledge right now: 'Whenever we have a prior inkling of fear, worry, disappointment, or any difficulty, we are going to laugh at ourselves.' Laughing at our mistakes and our silliness acts like a soothing lotion.

> Two friends were walking down the street. Suddenly, some bird droppings fell on one of them, soiling his shirt. His friend earnestly sympathized saying, 'Oh, this is bad! You are going for an interview; this shouldn't have happened with you.' The first one knew the secret of lightening the environment with laughter. He said, 'Thank God, it was only a crow. Just imagine if cows could fly! What would have been my condition?'

We meet a lot of people during the course of our day. Some of them have a higher tendency for anger than others. Anger is one of the ways of expressing one's inner thoughts. The more hatred a man carries inside him, the angrier he gets. On the other hand, someone with a laughing countenance has a lower incidence of anger. Our body is a mirror of our mind. As within, so without.

A man who is filled with joy will do everything with a smile and a laugh. He will stay cheerful and spread cheer, even when there are angry people in front of him. If someone throws stones at a fruit laden tree, the tree gives fruit in return. When clouds get filled with water, they shed rain, not fire. Likewise, whatever you are filled with, that is what you will give out. If someone is expressing his anger in front of you, but if you are filled with joy, then you will express joy.

To summarize, whatever you do, do it with a smile. When you spread happiness, you receive happiness in return. This is one of the laws of nature according to which: *Whatever you give, comes back to you.* If there is laughter from both sides, the possibility of anger is minimum.

Guest : Whenever I sit down to eat, your dog growls at me.

Host : Don't you worry; it's just that he recognizes his plate.

God : First know the truth.

Chapter 22

First Laughter And Discipline

Difference between laughing and crying

You need to be a little bit careful while carrying out the laughter experiment. Otherwise, someone may read this book and say, 'I read a book on laughter and laughed loudly in the classroom. The teacher punished me and made me cry!' Jokes apart, it is important to look at the place you are in, look at its environment, and only then laugh and listen to your laughter. Let us understand this through an example.

> A teacher saw two students fighting in her class and shouted, 'Don't fight! Live in harmony and help each other. Always remember this rule.' Hearing this, one of the students retorted, 'You are asking us to live in harmony and to help each other, but when we solve our test papers with each other's help, in harmony, you get very upset!'

This example demonstrates that the teacher is urging for cooperation with a good purpose in mind, while the student is asking permission for cooperation with a different goal in mind.

It is common sense to understand which school rule will apply under what circumstances. The rule of cooperation does not apply during examinations. Use a rule only where it is applicable. Drawing parallels, if someone gets disturbed with your laughter, do not try the laughter experiment before him.

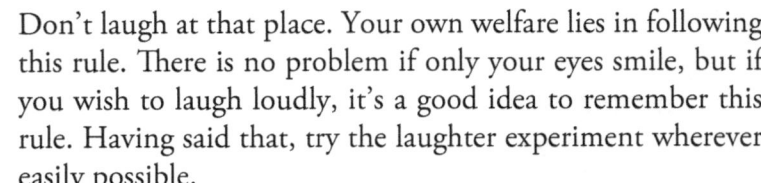

Don't laugh at that place. Your own welfare lies in following this rule. There is no problem if only your eyes smile, but if you wish to laugh loudly, it's a good idea to remember this rule. Having said that, try the laughter experiment wherever easily possible.

Become aware of your mistakes using your intellect, your understanding, and discrimination; and laugh at your blunders. How are you living your life? What do you consider yourself to be? Until now what were your beliefs about God, yourself, and your body? Realize your mistakes and laugh.

First true laughter

You laugh your first true laughter when you realize your ignorance.

> A truth seeker went to a master and said, 'Guruji, please give me knowledge.' The master said, 'In order to receive knowledge, you will have to perform an experiment. It is raining outside. Go out, look at the sky, and raise your hands for 2-3 minutes. Divine knowledge will automatically descend upon you.' The man was pleased. He went out, looked at the sky, and stood in the rain with his hands raised for 2-3 minutes. Suddenly, he felt amused. He started chuckling and went inside. The master asked, 'What happened? Why did you come in?' The man replied, 'When I was standing with my hands raised up in the rain, a thought occurred to me that I am looking so foolish standing like this! I am doing something so silly! I felt like laughing at myself and so I came in.'
>
> The master heard this and pronounced, 'This much knowledge is enough for one day. Today you have received an important understanding. You have become aware of your foolishness.'

In the same manner, when a swan comes to know that he has been leading his life considering himself to be an owl, he realizes his foolishness. That is the day when his first real laughter emerges. Let us understand this through an incident from the ancient times.

A man came across a monk who was the Buddha's follower. He asked the monk, 'You look quite old. What is your age?' The monk replied, 'I am five years old.' Taken aback by this answer, the man said, 'I thought you must be 60 or 70 years old but you say that you are only five years old! How's that possible?' The monk explained, 'Yes, I am five years old. The day the Buddha gave me knowledge, I laughed a real laughter for the first time. That was my first birthday. Five years have passed since then. Whatever was before that time was only an illusion.'

This incidence illustrates that there is a kind of laughter that emerges only after you attain wisdom. Your real life begins only after that. The illusory owl dies that day. The owl was just a false belief. The swan was considering itself to be an owl. When you learn this truth, you laugh your first true laughter.

How to do everything with a smile? What is meant by living with laughter? What is heart laughter? A little story will clarify these questions.

A doctor visited a village. Everyone in this village was scared of something or the other. Some people were scared of lizards, while others were afraid of grasshoppers. Some feared dogs, while others dreaded bears. There were some people who were frightened of all animals.

The doctor tried his best to cure them but to no avail. One day, he thought of a plan and declared, 'We shall organize a carnival. Everyone will wear a mask in this carnival. The moment you wear the mask, you will be free. You will be able to laugh openly. The mask will have one more advantage: the creature you fear will be in front of you but you won't fear it. Your fear will vanish forever. In addition, no one will recognize you because of the mask.'

The doctor's assistant measured everyone's faces and got the masks ready by the decided date. All the people arrived at the venue. The assistant himself put the masks on everyone's face one by one, without showing them what mask it was. Once this was done, the doctor announced, 'In this carnival, all of you have come wearing masks of lizards, grasshoppers, dogs, bears, etc. All these creatures are here that you get scared of. You have to play with only those creatures that you are afraid of. Now the music, singing, and dancing will begin.'

Everyone had their masks on and started singing and dancing. Who do you think laughed the loudest at this merry making? The doctor's assistant laughed the loudest because he knew who was hidden behind which mask. He had not divulged this secret to anyone, but he knew that the one jumping like a monkey was the one who was most scared of monkeys.

The day you see the real face behind your mask (the Unlimited Self beneath your body), real laughter will burst out from deep within your heart. When you realize that there is only one face behind all the masks, you will know what exactly heart laughter is.

Laughter of the heart

A saint asked his disciples, 'When does the night end and when does the morning begin? How do we recognize this? How will we know that the night has ended and ignorance has vanished?'

One of the disciples answered, 'When we have learnt the difference between a cow and a horse, it means that the night has ended.'

Another responded, 'When we know the difference between a neem tree and a mango tree, it indicates that the night has ended.'

A third one replied, 'When I see no difference between you and me, honour and dishonour, joy and sorrow, noise and silence, laughing and crying, Hindu and Muslim; it means the night has ended for me.' This answer was adjudged to be the right one.

There are many people in this world but there is only one entity behind all the masks, which can be seen only after the experience of the Truth. You have connected with this mask (i.e. body) to know and understand that experience of the Truth. Remember, this mask is not a bane, it is a boon. It becomes a bane only because of ignorance. We think we are the masks. We get attached to our mask. If someone throws muck on this mask, we think we have been soiled. This false belief makes us unhappy and puts a brake on our laughter. Do you feel sorrow when you car gets soiled? Not likely, because you know that you are not the car. In the same vein, think of your mask as your vehicle and always stay happy.

Beloved : I will always inspire you to laugh. I will share all your joys and sorrows.

Lover   : But I have no sorrow, I keep laughing all the time.

Beloved : I am talking about 'after' marriage.

God   : Beware before inviting sorrows into your life.

Section III
Special Compilation

'If you stay happy until ten in the morning,

the rest of the day will take care of itself.'
—Elbert Hubbard

'Prayer is when you talk to God;

Meditation is when you listen to God.'
—Diana Robinson

'Only he can laugh till the end,
who knows that there is no end.'

—Sirshree

Chapter 23

Expression of Laughter

Bliss is the nature of God. Laughter is His expression. Some of the other expressions of God through our bodies are in the form of hymns, songs, dancing, imparting discourses, writing discourses, rendering service, and so on. Laughter too is one of the various expressions of God through us. When you know your true self, this expression becomes easy for you.

We are already aware that the self-expression of man and animals is different from each other. Some people question as to why animals cannot laugh like humans, whereas they can cry like humans. The fact is that human and animal bodies express differently. However, whenever any body is under pressure, the pressure can make the eyes water. This is a natural method of releasing pressure from the body. God has made this arrangement. It is essential for physical health.

Women can cry easily and hence they get rid of their stress easily. Men accumulate stress and develop diseases due to their inability to cry freely. Tears release stress. Animals too use this tool. Whatever creates tension in animals, be it illness, environment or something else, they shed tears to relieve that tension. Animals live in an environment where danger from other animals is a constant reality. When they are free from danger, the stress is released and they become normal again.

If the tension in animals is because of the environment, their body automatically sheds tears and releases the tension. Animals do not think and cry. Neither, after the situation has passed, do they think, 'Why was I crying?' Tears appear spontaneously from their eyes and instantly release the tension. There is no thought process involved; it is just a bodily function which is helpful for the body in certain situations. But an animal cannot laugh because it cannot contemplate. Its body is not made in that manner. There is no possibility of an animal deciphering the Truth. This possibility lies only in man.

There is another question that people ask: 'Isn't it a curse for animals that God has made them mute?' No. We cannot understand their language and therefore think that animals are mute. Only man thinks that animals are mute, animals don't think so.

Please don't decide if dogs are mute or not… just ask a dog if its partner is mute. If you ask about a dog in its neighbourhood, they will tell you how much it barks. Barking is their language. They talk to each other in their own language. We think that only when they will speak like us, it will mean that they are not mute. This is our illusion. Nature has provided the freedom of various expressions to all species.

The same nature or God has endowed the highest tool of self-expression—laughter—to man, which is not possible in any other animal. Consider it as grace. Imbibe this boon of laughter in your life and keep laughing.

Professor : *Why do you leave in the middle of my class?*

Student: *Sir, actually, I have this problem of walking in my sleep.*

God : **Doubt the doubter; explore yourself by making others your mirror.**

Chapter 24

Laughter And Health

Laughter is a unique type of exercise and pranayam. It is a great exercise because it not only exercises your facial muscles and lungs but also resolves situations, problems, and improves relationships. Laughter is indeed a wonderful medicine for total health. When you laugh openly, all your organs get exercised. If you remain unhappy and worried, you invite many diseases. That is why you must face difficulties too with a smile and a laugh. Everyone feels good on meeting a jolly person. No one likes glum faces.

There are four ways in which we laugh. The first one is just smiling within. The second one is smiling through the lips, where the smile brings changes to the face alone. The third one is laughing with a sound, and the fourth one is guffawing loudly. Let us try all four whenever we can.

In today's stress filled era, man has forgotten to laugh. Take a pledge today itself that you will laugh and make your family laugh as well. Experts say that if you laugh loudly between 50-100 times, that is enough exercise for a day. If we cannot cure others' illnesses, we can at least help them recover faster by laughing and making them laugh.

There is a saying : 'Jolly people are full of life; sulky people are hardly alive.' There is a definite link between a patient's laughter and his health. Laughter enhances the life energy in the body. It elevates the number of white blood cells and reduces the level of blood cholesterol. When a man laughs openly and continuously for some time, his lungs get a fairly good exercise.

Laughter — a natural medicine

As you laugh, you stay joyful and also spread joy around you. A happy man can easily face all his troubles because his brain stays in balance. Laughter also improves digestion. It increases your physical capacity a great deal. Its effect is equal to running for a kilometre. Laughter is especially beneficial in blood pressure and cardiac problems. It also increases your enthusiasm for life. It is an easily available natural medicine.

Doctors too advise us to laugh. Ayurveda states that a hearty laughter creates vibrations in the entire energy system (*nadis*) of our body. This expels the impure air from our lungs. This also activates our muscles. Laughter is a natural remedy for stress, worries, frustration, pain, and suffering.

A happy man does not get angry. Only a morose man does. A happy man does not take any anger-inducing event seriously. He finds all events normal. Laughter softens us and purifies our mind. It clears the garbage collected from our past and gives us a new perspective towards life. It gives us a sense of being alive and makes us energetic and creative.

Medical science affirms that laughter prevents many diseases. In case someone is already suffering from an illness, he will be cured faster if he can laugh.

Anger, fear, and hatred are mental illnesses, of which laughter is the sure-fire cure. Today doctors are healing many mental illnesses with laughter therapy. If you start your day with laughter, you will experience a stress-free life. Early morning laughter prevents you from being grim throughout the day. It is a beautiful way to begin a day. Just as you eat three meals a day, you must laugh at least three times without any cause. If you can do that, the vibration of happiness will stay with you the entire day. Anger will stay miles away from you, even in the face of an unpleasant situation. If you laugh in the morning, you will feel like laughing the whole day.

Don't laugh only through your lips, head or belly; laugh through your heart and become a swan. One happy man can accomplish more than a hundred whining men.

Father : *What are you drying in the sun?*
Son : *My sweat.*
God : In ignorance, you lose more than you gain.

Divine Guidance

1. Interpret the meaning hidden in words, don't get stuck in words.
2. Listen carefully before answering and don't try to act too smart.
3. Do not use shortcuts for learning the Truth.
4. A doctor should heal himself first or heal himself in parallel while treating others.
5. Throw the umbrella and wake up.
6. It is easy to remain unconscious. Consciousness is difficult but essential.
7. Don't look for owls; look for swans.
8. Don't be a slave of wrong habits.
9. Don't just laugh; correct your mistakes too.
10. Turn around; where is your attention? On the letter, the writer, or the postman?
11. Don't make assumptions; listen completely. Turn your mind within.
12. Are the political leaders, lawyers, doctors, and teachers of today losing the trait of honesty? If so, please revive it.

13. Whatever you do, do it with a smile.
14. Please don't make any presumptions about God.
15. People remain stuck in illusion even after hearing the truth.
16. Teasing someone is not true laughter.
17. A foolish man's logic increases foolishness. A fool's company can even prove fatal.
18. Don't misuse your intellect. Don't imbibe substances that corrupt your intellect.
19. Search for your true laughter.
20. No reason is required for laughter. Only your presence is required.
21. First know the truth.
22. Beware before inviting sorrows into your life.
23. Doubt the doubter; explore yourself by making others your mirror.
24. In ignorance, you lose more than you gain.

You can mail your opinion or feedback on this book to:
books.feedback@tejgyan.org

APPENDICES

About Sirshree

Sirshree's spiritual quest, which began during his childhood, led him on a journey through various schools of philosophy and meditation practices. He studied a wide range of literature on mind science and spirituality. After a long period of deep contemplation on the truth of life, his quest culminated in attaining the ultimate truth.

Sirshree espouses, "All spiritual paths that lead to the truth begin differently but culminate at the same point – Understanding. This understanding is complete in itself. Listening to this understanding is enough to attain the Truth." Over the last two decades, he has dedicated his life to raise mass consciousness.

Sirshree has delivered more than 4000 discourses that throw light on this understanding. He has designed a system for wisdom, which makes it accessible to all. This system has inspired people from all walks of life to progress on their journey of the Truth. Thousands of seekers join in a virtual prayer for World Peace and Global Healing daily at 9:09 am and 9:09 pm.

About Tej Gyan Foundation

Tej Gyan Foundation is a non-profit organization founded on the teachings of Sirshree. The Foundation disseminates Tejgyan – the wisdom that guides one from self-development to Self-realization, leading towards Self-stabilization.

The Foundation's system for imparting wisdom has been assessed by international quality auditors and accredited with the ISO 9001:2015 certification. This wisdom has been presented in a simple, systematic, and practically applicable form that makes it accessible to people from all walks of life, regardless of religion, caste, social strata, country, or belief system.

The Foundation has centers in more than 400 cities and towns across India and other countries. The mission of Tej Gyan Foundation is to create a highly evolved society by leading seekers from negative thoughts to positive thoughts and further, from positive thoughts to Happy thoughts. A 'Happy thought' is the auspicious thought of being free from all thoughts, leading to the state of supreme bliss beyond thoughts.

If you seek such wisdom that leads you beyond mere knowledge, dissolves all problems, frees you from all limiting beliefs, reveals the true nature of divinity, and establishes you in the ultimate truth, then it is time to discover Tejgyan; it is time to rise above the mundane knowledge of words and experience Tejgyan!

The MahaAasmani Magic of Awakening Retreat

Self-development to Self-realization towards Self-stabilization

Do you wish to experience unconditional happiness that is not dependent on any reason? Happiness that is permanent and only increases with time? Do you wish to experience love, peace, self-belief, harmony in relationships, prosperity, and true contentment? Do you wish to progress in all facets of your life, viz. physical, mental, social, financial, and spiritual?

If you seek answers to these questions and are thirsty for the ultimate truth, then you are welcome to participate in the MahaAasmani Magic of Awakening retreat organized by Tej Gyan Foundation. This is the Foundation's flagship retreat based on the teachings of Sirshree.

The purpose of this retreat

The purpose of this retreat is that every human being should:

- Discover the answer to "Who am I" and "Why am I?" through direct experience and be established in ultimate bliss.

- Learn the art of living in the present, free from the burden of the past and the anxiety of the future.

- Acquire practical tools to help quieten the chattering mind and dissolve problems.

- Discover missing links in the practices of Meditation (*Dhyana*), Action (*Karma*), Wisdom (*Gyana*), and Devotion (*Bhakti*).

About Books by Sirshree

Sirshree's published work includes more than 150 book titles, some of which have been translated into more than 10 languages. His literature provides a profound reading on various topics of practical living and unravels the missing links in karma, wisdom, devotion, meditation, and consciousness.

His books have been published by leading publishing houses like Penguin, Hay House, Bloomsbury, Wisdom Tree, Jaico, etc. "The Source" book series, authored by Sirshree, has sold over 10 million copies. Various luminaries and celebrities like His Holiness the Dalai Lama, publishers Mr. Reid Tracy, Ms. Tami Simon and Yoga Master Dr. B. K. S. Iyengar have released Sirshree's books and lauded his work.

The Source
Attain Both, Inner Peace
and Worldly success

Awaken the Power of Faith
Discover the 7 Principles of the
Highest Power of the Universe

To order books authored by Sirshree, login to:
www.gethappythoughts.org
For further details, call: +91 9011013210

Tej Gyan Foundation – Contact details

Registered Office:
Happy Thoughts Building, Vikrant Complex, Near Tapovan Mandir, Pimpri, Pune 411017, INDIA. Contact: +91 20-27411240, +91 20-27412576

MaNaN Ashram:
Survey No. 43, Sanas Nagar, Nandoshi Gaon, Kirkatwadi Phata, Off Sinhagad Road, Taluka Haveli, Pune district - 411024, INDIA. Contact: +91 992100 8060.

WORLD PEACE PRAYER

Divine Light of Love, Bliss, and Peace is Showering;

The Golden Light of Higher Consciousness is Rising;

All negativity on Earth is Dissolving;

Everyone is in Peace and Blissfully Shining;

O God, Gratitude for Everything!

Members of Tej Gyan Foundation have been offering this impersonal mass prayer for many years. Those who are happy can offer this prayer. Those feeling low or suffering from illness can receive healing with this prayer.

If you are feeling troubled or sick, please sit to receive the healing effect of this prayer. Visualize that the divine white healing light is being showered on earth through the prayers of thousands and is also reaching you, bringing you peace and good health. You can dwell in this feeling for some time and then offer your gratitude to those offering the prayer.

A Humble Appeal

More than a million peace lovers pray for World Peace and Global Healing every morning and evening at 9:09. Also, a prayer (in Hindi) to elevate consciousness is webcast every day on YouTube at 3:30 pm and 9:00 pm IST. Please participate in this noble endeavor.

www.ingramcontent.com/pod-product-compliance
Lightning Source LLC
LaVergne TN
LVHW041848070526
838199LV00045BA/1502